CUNARD

❖

Library

Out of respect for your fellow guests, please return all books as soon as possible. We would also request that books are not taken off the ship as they can easily be damaged by the sun, sea and sand.

Please ensure that books are returned the day before you disembark, failure to do so will incur a charge to your on board account, the same will happen to any damaged books.

www.oceanbooks.com

The Gift of a Radio

www.penguin.co.uk

The Gift of a Radio

My Childhood and other Train Wrecks

Justin Webb

doubleday

TRANSWORLD PUBLISHERS
Penguin Random House, One Embassy Gardens,
8 Viaduct Gardens, London SW11 7BW
www.penguin.co.uk

Transworld is part of the Penguin Random House group of companies
whose addresses can be found at global.penguinrandomhouse.com

First published in Great Britain in 2022 by Doubleday
an imprint of Transworld Publishers

A CIP catalogue record for this book
is available from the British Library.

ISBN 9780857527721

Typeset in 12/15.5 pt Minion by Jouve (UK), Milton Keynes
Printed and bound in Great Britain by Clays Ltd, Elcograf S.p.A.

The authorized representative in the EEA is Penguin Random House Ireland,
Morrison Chambers, 32 Nassau Street, Dublin D02 YH68.

Penguin Random House is committed to a sustainable
future for our business, our readers and our planet. This book
is made from Forest Stewardship Council® certified paper.

To Mum and Charles

'If others examined themselves attentively, as I do, they would find themselves, as I do, full of inanity and nonsense. Get rid of it I cannot without getting rid of myself. We are all steeped in it, one as much as another, but those who are aware of it are a little better off – though I don't know.'

Michel de Montaigne

Contents

All at Sea

A week after her wedding day, Mum made an appointment with our GP, rumpled, ginger-haired, stethoscope-wearing Dr Neil, because Charles, her new life partner, my new stepfather, had poured all the milk down the sink. Charles told her that he thought it had been tampered with and Mum felt this might be something that a doctor needed to hear about. Dr Neil was on it: his response perfectly caught the tone of the times.

'Mrs Webb: I regret to inform you that your husband is stark staring mad.'

And so it all began. For her, for him, for me. No one is to blame for what followed. Far from it. Coping is an under-praised virtue. And coping in the 1970s deserves special recognition. I look back not in anger but in amazement. Each decade has its challenges and there have been far tougher, odder childhoods than mine. But for confusion, for angst, for the clash of tidal forces ready to knock you off your feet, no postwar decade comes close. We were all at sea in the seventies. Often out of our depth, bobbing around, going under.

So it's fitting, I suppose, that my own memories start at the water's edge. It's a few years after Dr Neil's diagnosis. I'm six, maybe seven years old. My stepfather has announced that he is to bathe before we go home from our day trip to the beach. Bathe. Not swim. We live in a world of distressed gentlefolk pretension. He gets up from his towel and pushes back his hair. He is a handsome man of medium build; he has longish hair that needs to be pushed back frequently or oiled and parted vigorously with a plastic comb before he goes to work. Today it sticks up and gives him a Viking swagger.

He strides to the shoreline and stops, as strong swimmers sometimes do, to contemplate the waves. Then he walks, then he dives. Now he's resurfaced and his arms begin their lazy loops through the water. A bit of crawl. On to the back. A couple of powerful butterfly strokes. He's out to sea. Deep into Lulworth Cove. He seems further out than the rock. Within minutes he's a pinprick. If I hold my finger at arm's length from my eye he disappears. Mum's next to me. My spade is at rest and the sandcastle abandoned. (Something was always missing that would have made sandcastle-building fun. I did it out of duty. Mum inspected them perfunctorily, not knowing what she was looking for.) We are both squinting into the sun, looking at my stepfather swimming further and further out. The water is flat-calm but deep where he is now. There will be currents, rip tides. Out and out he goes.

And then he comes back.

Many decades have passed but I remember the feeling I had at that moment with vividness undimmed. I was disappointed. There's no other word. It wasn't hatred or anger or petulance. I was too young to think about the consequences, good or bad, of the actual body being dragged out of the waves and worked on and declared dead. But I formed in that instant the considered opinion that it would have been better if he had drowned. Better for me. Better for her. Better for us. We were together, Mum and I, but we had been joined by him. He was never Dad except in formal letters home from school. At home he was Charles. 'Mummy,' I had asked her once, when I was small: 'Where did we get Charles?' I suggested she went to the pub and got another, superior man. The idea made her laugh. She repeated it often. Inside, though, I think it made her cry. And she was never able to answer my question. It hung there like so much else hung over us through my childhood.

Of course, I didn't actually think of killing him myself that day and he did not actually die. But the disappointment felt like a wet little crime of its own. A slithery thing that only I could feel, like seaweed in the bathing trunks. Could others see it? Could they sense me moving oddly, shifting uncomfortably? Perhaps. It was an ongoing crime: I had the feeling for years to come. People can commit adultery in their minds, and murder, too. You don't have to act on it to feel the guilt.

On the journey home to Bath, in the Hillman Minx with no radio, the three of us were silent. We always travelled in silence but this was deeper. I sat in the back, digging out sand from under my fingernails. The normal tension of the car journey had another layer: I knew what I had thought. And I didn't mind that I had thought it.

That tension in the car was always overlaid with fear. Charles couldn't stand driving behind anyone and overtook constantly, dangerously. 'What *is* this man doing?' he asked through clenched teeth as we lurched, gears crunching, into the centre of the road for an engine-gunning, flat-out, whites-of-their-eyes race into the path of an oncoming lorry, before pulling back into our lane, just in time. I knew what I'd thought. Acknowledging it brought an odd kind of peace.

Charles didn't deserve to die. I don't think he contemplated murdering me or my mother or anyone else. The impact of mental distress is often oblique, not direct. It saps and undermines. It didn't hit me or chase me (and he never did, either) but it lived with me, in my head as much as in his. Charles was a damaged man living with a damaged woman and a damaged child in an era when all mental illness was regarded with a mixture of fear and hilarity. As a reaction to this – and with still more ghastly results – it was being reinvented as mundane, even, ironically, 'normal'. Maybe it didn't even exist, chirruped those who claimed to be liberated. This was, after all, the era of 'anti-psychiatry', in which madness was going to be magically reduced to nothing much to worry about. So-called psychiatric survivor movements sought to vindicate those who might think of themselves as justified in their choice of thoughts; any thoughts, whatever they were, could be valid, welcome at the table.

Some of the arguments of the anti-psychiatrists were highly seductive. Schizophrenia – in those days a blanket term that had little real meaning – did not involve any obvious physical changes to the brain. So was it real? Was it in the minds of those diagnosing it as much as the alleged sufferers from the condition? When the Scottish psychoanalyst R. D. Laing told us that schizophrenia was 'a sane reaction to an insane world', many people were hearing something they wanted to believe. It seemed to be a liberation to go alongside the burning of bras or the refusal to serve in Vietnam.

Deconstruction of all things was freedom. Nothing mattered unless you said it did. Nothing mattered unless it mattered to you. Nothing was real outside your mind. Just as the American hippies were chipping away at objective truth, psychiatry was facing a wave of mad and unhappy people intent on doing it in.

Few people remember R. D. Laing these days, but just to labour the point: I am here to tell you that nothing he said is true. And the biggest lie of all was that mental illness was a natural by-product of social order, of the pressures of the nuclear family. Laing suggested to a gullible post-1960s intelligentsia that the schizophrenic was often the scapegoat of a dysfunctional family and was, paradoxically, the sanest person in the family group: 'Without exception the experience and behaviour that gets labelled as schizophrenia is a special strategy that the patient invents in order to live with an unliveable situation.'

My own family life was a grasshopper under the wheel of one of those oncoming lorries that Charles used to dodge in the car. With nowhere to jump to, we were crushed. Charles's illness was not created by our wan little nuclear gathering. The opposite: the illness destroyed our family as a unit.

It happened, I'm pretty sure, on day seven, the day Mum visited the doctor with her news about the milk. She had married Charles in 1963, a couple of years after having me, and hoped that her troubles were over. She and I would be cared for in a world before women had full control of their affairs, a world of profound danger for a single mother; and for women in general, in which untalked-about things lurked in unmentionable places. That same year, 1963, the Duke and Duchess of Argyll divorced; at the heart of the case, which caused a sensation, were photos of something she was doing to someone. Christine Keeler went to jail. Oh, and a Soviet woman went into orbit. Quite possibly to escape.

Dr Neil understood that distress of the mind destroyed everything in its path. His approach to it was that of a man with a stethoscope hearing an unwelcome echo in a dodgy lung. There was no need for histrionics but no need, either, for euphemism or obfuscation. You had to find the words for it. Stark staring was, he felt, as good a term as any. But, unlike an infirmity picked up by his stethoscope or a quick feel of some swollen part of you, madness was a bit of a head-scratcher. There were all sorts of wacky ideas around but, even in the world of conventional medicine, no real options far removed from the placing of leeches.

There was talk of electric-shock therapy for Charles but it never happened. Nor was he ever really threatened with being locked up. The upside of the anti-psychiatry move-ment was its challenging of the old ways of 'treating' mental illness. They had nothing to put in place of the old ways but the old ways were usually useless and often more harmful than just leaving well alone, so, on balance, it was progress.

Charles was left well alone. He took Valium for the rest of his life and Mum and I tried to carry on as if everything on the medical front was fine or copeable with. It wasn't; not really, not ever. But we carried on anyway.

One of the immediate impacts of illness of the mind is a separation between the person in whose mind things have gone haywire and everyone else. My mother never talked to me about her 'relationship' with Charles (she would have rolled her eyes at the word), but putting the story together years later it's obvious that the kind of bed-rock of which long, stable marriages are made could not have been built in these early years. He'd begun by pouring the milk down the sink. Then, months later, he started getting up in the small hours and playing Bach on the record-player that stood in a cabinet in the sitting room. At maximum volume.

In a small, modern, end-of-terrace house this cannot be a secret vice; indeed, I think the whole point was to alert people. But to what? I remember no firm answer – nothing explained even *sotto voce* – but part of his illness expressed itself as a kind of persecution complex which told him constantly that people looked down on him. As far as Charles was concerned, his intellect was the butt of a continuous nationwide joke. The authorities thought he was a loser. The neighbours agreed (they did, I expect, but cause and effect became confused in the circumstances). His answer was to show them that they were wrong. Hence Bach, whose presence in our home revealed panache, a certain degree of learning and a hinterland no one on our estate could match.

Looking back, I wonder if the situation didn't make us all a little bit mad, as the trendies suggested. In a dysfunctional age, we could hold our heads high, Charles and Mum and I. We were properly screwed up. In the modern world we've become used to the idea of survival rates. What were the chances of survival from my house? I don't mean of not dying. I mean of escaping into the 1980s as a semi-functional adult? Also, to employ a term we all got used to when COVID-19 hit, what is the 'R' number for these multiple small sadnesses? The reproduction number: the rate at which they are passed on. If there is no vaccine against childhood misery, can there at least be a treatment that stops it cascading through the decades, the centuries? Or is there something rather glorious about the randomness of everything that happens to us?

~

My mother, Gloria Crocombe, was a small, dark woman, short-haired, round-cheeked and busy. She had been born, in 1924, into great comfort and, along with her siblings – Oliver, slightly younger, and Charmion, slightly older – lived a life of gradually diminishing privilege. A large rented house in Walton-on-Thames. A cook and a maid called Dolly. A driver to take them on picnics on the Sussex Downs, who would wait in the car while they ate. Then the war, the loss of servants and tightness of funds. Schooling at first interrupted and eventually terminated. University out of the question, still, for most girls, even those gently born. And a diminished shell-shocked world awaiting them. Yes, there were balls and there was booze. There was still a large army into which my Uncle Oliver subsided via Sandhurst. But there was, too, a general reduction in life chances. There was a reckoning, inescapable even for those who survived the war itself. A reckoning that went on for decades, far into the 1970s, a folk memory of collapse that haunted us when we headed for civil strife so soon after the guns had been silenced.

So none of the early comforts of life had been passed down the generations: postwar austerity and the divorce of the parents saw to that. Their father had been a big noise in magazines, but when he left his wife, he took the money, too. I realize now that Mum had been reinventing herself when I was young. Her early adult life was a mystery to me. There had been dissolute behaviour, though. Boys, men, drink. There had been a period in her twenties when she'd lived in the Home Counties with her first husband and drunk with Petula Clark before she was famous. It was an aspect of her character that she never revealed a word more than necessary and a developing feature of mine that I never asked.

At some point there had been visits to Spielplatz, a retreat in Hertfordshire where people don't wear clothes. And affairs that ended poorly. A man she loved – she never used that word about anything as frivolous as male–female relationships, but it seemed to fit – had taken her on holiday in some respite from postwar austerity. It was a proper holiday, to the south of France, still recovering from the war and as exotic then as the deepest Amazon would be now. They had come back on the luxury sleeper known as the Blue Train that in those days ran from Nice to Calais, across the Channel on the ferry and on to London, where he promptly vomited blood and died at Victoria station.

It was never clear whether this was an unexpected end to an otherwise idyllic trip or whether the whole event was a goodbye, a tragedy ending in the denouement at the station. I was too fastidious to probe. When you have a show to keep on the road you don't go to places that might jeopardize the balance of mind of the leading lady.

So I know little either about her first husband, married on the rebound from this traumatic train journey. He was called Stewart and had one leg. The other had been blown off in Palestine. He drank too much and they soon divorced. What happened to him? Did they stay in touch? She never said. I have never found any letters. And then, in the foothills of middle age (she was thirty-six when she had me), she made a decision to devote herself to her child and to seriousness. Her past became another country to her. She became a Quaker. She decided that nuclear weapons were evil. But she also thought our neighbours were common, lower-middle class. She mocked the way they called in their girls for their evening meal: 'Alisern!' 'Rachil!' Ghastly names, she said without saying. Mispronounced, too. You clipped the vowels. Alisn. Rachl. My mother talked like an announcer on the prewar Home Service. Throughout her life – through all the changes – she remained ineffably snobbish.

But she could be such fun, too. She got humour. The Cambridge Footlights stuff that was the best of the telly in the 1960s made her guffaw. Her favourite was Peter Cook's miner's monologue that began, 'I could have been a judge, but I never 'ad the Latin. I never 'ad the Latin for the judgin'.'

She was on the side of the judges. We seemed to have the Latin. We were in on the joke and we had our own defensive laughter at the outside world. Once, when I was young and we couldn't go on a coach trip because we had run out of money, she said, gravely, 'But we can pay our bills.'

'Ah yes,' I mocked, 'I bet we can and I bet we will.'

She loved that.

But when it came to it, she wanted me cut loose from the house, with its sinews of sadness, before any bills, or bailiffs, came. I sometimes wonder if my mother included herself in the list of things from which I should flee. There were times when she acted like those women in war films who throw their babies into the backs of trucks to save them from otherwise certain death. She wanted me gone, for both our sakes. It was a calamitous instinct. It hurt her and me. The baby in the truck doesn't always get looked after by kindly strangers and the mother left behind doesn't always get the satisfaction of seeing the child fly away towards freedom. The soldiers came anyway for Mum and me, and half got us both.

Everything I've ever learned about being a man I learned from a woman. This is not ideal. My mother was born at a time when middle-class women – outside the Bloomsbury set – were housewives or autodidacts with lifestyles funded by pipe-smoking chaps with jobs in the City. She never managed either. She hankered rather pathetically after men, then hated their guts, then regarded them with contempt before sliding back into longing.

She fucked me up just as Philip Larkin said she would.

But she bore out, too, the deeper truth of that often fleetingly quoted poem. She herself was fucked up in her time by 'fools in old-style hats and coats'. The misery (and joy) she passed to me was distilled from a previous age.

Something else, though, was afoot. Mum often declared, in self-mocking tones that suggested she knew it was silly but wanted it to be true, that the world was my oyster. But I already knew this. I had a feeling about where I belonged that was entirely, mysteriously, out of kilter with where I actually was.

All of this took place at a time of quite mind-boggling cultural and social collapse. We think of our own fractured age as the Olympics of disaster, the very pinnacle of End Times. Nothing, we tend to believe as we fret about social media and climate change and pandemics and populism, could ever match this degree of dislocation of everything, of social decay and political stasis. At least, nothing outside war. Well, it did. The 1970s were still close to a war – you could reach back and touch it – but this era had worked up, by the middle of the decade, a peacetime cataclysm of its own. Things had fallen down. Those things that still stood were flying apart. There was talk of 'wholesale domestic liquidation': the collapse of every British company, brought on by just one or two leading firms going to the wall.

At the same time, according to Joe Haines, then press secretary to the prime minister, Harold Wilson, Wilson's private doctor was suggesting that the prime minister ought to consider murdering his political secretary, Marcia Williams, who may or may not have been blackmailing her boss. Wilson himself was wondering if he might be able to assassinate another world leader, Uganda's Idi Amin. Ministers who went abroad used to come home with groceries, bags of sugar and flour, in case rationing came back. Jimmy Savile was more than an advertiser of trains. He was in his pomp. On *Top of the Pops*. Visiting Broadmoor. We were children in a very adult decade.

When I was eleven, I wrote to *Woman's Hour* about rape. The letter was read out. I listened in my bedroom, with Mum, to my actual words being spoken by Sue MacGregor. We sat on the bed. It was summer and the thin, metal-framed windows were open. The diesel trains on the London to Bristol line at the bottom of the garden thrashed and fumed. The city of Bath hummed as small cities do on hot summer days – traffic in the distance, birds in our garden. Perhaps there were children playing. In my mind's eye there is some kind of familiar cacophony but it pauses, suddenly, when Sue MacGregor reads my words, as if a conductor has taken control and raised his baton.

In that moment, everything stood still. Life would restart, but it would be different. It would have shape and purpose. My words, each one weighed and considered and thumped into vivid inky life on Basildon Bond paper rolled into the guts of the huge black hardly portable typewriter Mum had bought me for Christmas. A typewriter on which, if you got excited and banged 't' 'h' 'e' with too much aplomb, the keys would jam together and have to be unstuck. Sue MacGregor, prim, still an ingénue herself, doing justice to those typed *mots justes*. Guided by them. Guided by me. Eleven years old, breaking free, starting out.

Her task wasn't, in truth, very difficult. The letter was punchy. Not all men were rapists, I said, and I would be grateful if this fact could be noted.

That was it. In a previous programme, there had been a discussion about sexual violence during which I'd gained the impression that Sue MacGregor thought all men were at it. Which somehow included me. I had asked for my name to be withheld but supplied it anyway, and the address, 90 Wells Road, Bath, so that the letter could be used: God knows how I was aware that this convention existed.

I certainly wasn't aware of what rape was, and Mum didn't want to tell me. I had surmised that it was quite wrong and more common than it should be. It plainly involved men and women and was imposed by the former on the latter. As such it fitted into a picture of society, of life, that Mum was painting but that, even at this young age, I felt I needed to elude.

Too late. In so many respects. Except perhaps one: I knew nothing about rape but I knew, that day, about desire. I knew about one boy's uncontrollable urges: I wanted to say things and have them read to people. Anything, anyone. I wanted to correct the record. Perhaps to create it. I wanted to catch the attention of people outside the strange little box near the railway line that was my 'family home'.

That radio, by the way, on which this early triumph had been registered, had come at Christmas. It was not a surprise. It was too weighty a purchase to be frivolously gifted. It had been *discussed*. My stepfather had been involved, as he had to be in all matters of accounting. *Which?* magazine had been consulted. And the winner at the end of the discussions was: the ITT Tiny Super. Portable but with proper sound in case I should one day wish to listen to classical music. Tone, Mum called it. The first thing I heard on it, turning the dial to 247 medium wave, Radio 1, was Harry Nilsson.

'I can't live if living is without you . . .'

I sat with tears in my eyes while Mum fiddled with the oven. I knew that one day she would be gone. And, as I've said, there was no one else. Except, now, the radio. Radio connects as nothing else does. It leaps over the barriers of loneliness. It scoops you up. It takes you with it. You need do nothing. You don't have to listen, still less respond. It will be there when you come back again. It will be there when you want it. When you need it. It forgives you your silence, your gaucheness, your absence. When you put it by your ear, it will speak directly to you. That, in the seventies, in no particular order, meant Emperor Rosko, William Hardcastle, Tony Blackburn, Jimmy Young, *The Archers*, Denis Norden on *My Word!*.

It was quite a gift.

I suppose I should mention my actual biological father, too. He made an appearance at home via a black-and-white TV – a flatter medium from which nothing good comes – shortly after we bought a guinea pig. Events fade and merge when you're young. Sorting out their importance comes later. Or perhaps it's the opposite: perhaps we attribute importance to things in accordance with our adult prejudices about what should and should not be. Perhaps we were right as kids: the guinea pig mattered as much. Anyway, it happened like this. The TV news came on and a lugubrious-looking chap in a light-coloured suit with a deep, plummy voice said something about the balance of payments. 'That's your father,' my mother said, quite unprompted. I don't think I spoke. I looked at the balance of payments, which seemed to be a concern. The position was worsening for reasons that were even more unclear to me than they were to the wider, collapsing, nation.

I had a red teddy bear – a handmade stuffed thing with black wool strands for hair. Some time after the balance of payments evening I named it Peter. But we were very grown-up about the real Peter Woods. We hardly mentioned him again.

As I said, nobody will be blamed here except, perhaps, me, for not asking the questions that demand answers decades later. But we live in an age that has fooled itself into thinking the answers are obvious if only the nitwits in charge, or on Twitter, or in universities or newspapers, could get their acts together and think things through properly.

The 1970s were properly complicated. Perhaps there are lessons for us all in the rear-view mirror.

And that's not the point anyway. The opposite, in fact: this is a small account of survival, of coming of age and saying goodbye to bad times, not of finger-pointing in the modern way. There was a crash in the end. But I survived. Before that there was a lot of swerving. The swerving was everything.

2

Don't Say What, Say Pardon

We are in my mother and stepfather's bedroom in a cul-de-sac called The Beeches on the outskirts of the city of Bath. It is the late 1960s. Mum and Charles still slept together, or at least in the same room. They are going out for the evening. He's already downstairs checking arrangements. She's dressing. I am lying on the floor, playing with toy cars and with her shoes that have been scattered around the bed.

'They're boats,' I say. 'Look at the boats!' In my game the shoes are sailing across the brightly coloured carpet, each puce or magenta clutch of manmade fibre a glistening wave.

But she has been applying hairspray and is distracted.

'Boats!' she exclaims in mock horror that actually isn't mock at all. 'No! You mean *boots*. Don't say boats. Say "boots"! Boats is . . .' A slight pause. 'Horrible.'

'But I meant to say boats. I mean the boots are boats. Boats on the sea.'

We fall about. She hugs me. It's the funniest thing that has ever happened in The Beeches. Tensions that cannot be guessed at by a boy are released. I remember it as a moment of giddy gaiety. A disaster – a mispronunciation disaster, a class disaster – had been narrowly averted. The misunderstanding was a perfectly formed comedy sketch. It needed timing and execution. It had a shape and a final triumphant climax. It had pathos. It had two players and needed no more. The audience, the two players, appreciated it exquisitely, viscerally.

But beneath the waters so much stirred that wasn't really funny at all. My mother's prejudices were more than skin deep. A dislike of slack-jawed people who said 'boats' when they meant 'boots' was the very tip of an iceberg fathomless and solid enough to sink a thousand ships. I sailed my whole life in its wake. My mother lived on the ice.

This was a vivacious and loving woman, a person who smiled and laughed easily; in later life a person who thought deeply about ethics, who spoke Spanish, wrote letters to prisoners of conscience for Amnesty International, who loved the poetry of William Carlos Williams, who admired modern art. And yet a woman who saw the entire world through the prism of social class. Really: the whole world. All of Creation. You had to be there.

We misunderstand snobbism, those of us who have survived and lived into modernity. We imagine it to be, in postwar England, an elephant in the room whose presence gradually faded as the 1960s got underway and Michael

Caine prospered and satire blossomed; the whole experience a uniformly felt reduction in class tension as working-
class heroes became something to be.

But no: bugger Michael Caine, as Mum might have said
(words with shock value were unbanned), because for
Mum, the attitudes that powered her early life remained
with her into the gloom and collapse, the flared trousers
and glam rock, the miners' strike, decimalization, Monty
Python: all of the social whirlpool of the seventies took
place in the lee of class. It was not going anywhere. It was
not an elephant in the room: it was the whole room. From
light fittings to couch. The couch that could not be called
the couch. Or even the sofa. In our home it was the 'divan'
with a slight accent on the 'aan' bit. We mapped out the world,
re-envisioning, re-christening, re-imagining it through a
lens into which other, lesser people could not gaze. Nothing could alter it. Education wouldn't help. Good character
was irrelevant. As was bad. Money could come and go and
not a jot of status would change.

My mother lived in a world of caste. She was at the top
because she said she was born there. There was nothing
genteel about her snobbery, no chink in her armour. Not
for her the tentative and pleading holding out of the little
finger from the grasp of a teacup. No twitch of the curtains
that suggested anything approaching self-doubt or any
kind of nervousness at all. This was not a Hyacinth Bucket
lifestyle. When it came to right and wrong, socially, there
was no nagging doubt, no hesitation: she was right and you

were likely to be wrong. When the Queen opened up Buckingham Palace to the cameras, Mum thought it common.

'Don't say what, say pardon' was a catchphrase relished in our house, a ready drawbridge to be hauled up when the moment dictated that the outside world should be put in its place and our own intense bond strengthened. This injunction had been heard in the mouths of our despised neighbours, the Burgesses, the parents of my playmates Alison and Rachel. By now we had downsized from The Beeches and bought a home closer to the city though still very much on the wrong side of the Bath tracks. There were three little houses together: ours was one of the end ones. In the middle were the Burgesses. They were normal, decent, striving folk. She was a nervy, birdlike housewife and he did the accounts for a company in Chippenham, which required a daily short train journey and would lead to a respectable final salary pension. He took sandwiches to work. This was not quite the era of bank clerks but still there was a cadre of white-collar workers who were not really properly white-collar, not running anything but not getting their hands dirty, either. I think he was called Bob. On Saturdays he played rugby.

Their sin, the Burgesses, was their indeterminate, perhaps advancing, status. They were not properly working class. In fact, they seemed to think they were better – in my mother's unyielding estimation – than they actually were. The words 'lower-middle class' reverberated around our home whenever the Burgesses stuck their neat little heads out of their tightly fitting front door.

And when, across the mean, wiry little fence that separated our back gardens, that disastrous utterance from Burgess parent to Burgess child had been made in my mother's earshot, it was a moment of triumph that confirmed everything.

She loved it even more hugely because the girl being upbraided had probably said 'what' after hearing it from me. We, of course, would never have said anything else but 'what'. People who said 'pardon' were the very lowest of the low. It was a chintzy foreign word, substituted by the lower orders (Mum used that term with no hint of irony) for a manly English one in the hope of inveigling their way into a place in which they did not belong. Oh, how my mum found you out, you blighters. Cut you back down. Good luck, suckers. Keep feeding your children this pernicious lesson and see whether they ever get anywhere.

In later life the Burgess girls probably used perfume. Again oblivious to what the anglicization of a French word does to your position in society. 'Perfume' is scent. Or *parfum*, if you are in France. It is a word I remember being banned very early and with striking firmness. So I said 'what' and, later, when it became relevant, 'scent'. In time, as the body begins to wear out, I may need dentures. But that's a French word: utterly vile and literally unspeakable. False teeth are false teeth.*

---

* To this day I cannot utter those words so terrible that it is difficult even to commit them to the page. When I see 'toilet' in a BBC script I cross it out and put 'loo'.

Curled up in bed one day with an encyclopaedia, I came across a shocking discovery which I could not pass on but kept, samizdat-like, bookmarked for posterity. I read that the word 'window' originates from the Old Norse 'vindauga', from 'vindr' (wind) and 'auga' (eye). Wind eye. This, of course, raised some issues. Was it OK to use a Norse word, a word brought over from the continent and anglicized? How does 'window' differ from 'perfume'? Worse: we had a perfectly good word of our own, or our ancestors did. *Eagþyrl*. Eyehole, to you and me. How many eons must pass before the use of a foreign word no longer looks like minor-league social climbing? Did Olde Englande have lower-middle-class people in it? A chink in Mum's armour had appeared. 'Don't say eyehole, say vindauga!'

At least the Vikings were assertive. People talk about snobs wanting to live in polite society: we certainly did not. Because politesse itself was for minor-league people. We admired bluntness. Gruffness. Language that forces open doors. Puts people on the defensive. Creates a hierarchy with you at the top. Mum was smilier than the Duke of Edinburgh but had the same general demeanour.

How does one watch television when one is upper-middle class? The question was never posed in quite those terms, of course, but the introduction of a rented TV set to 90 Wells Road was a big and difficult moment. First, it had to be discreet. The black-and-white set was placed at an angle in a corner behind an armchair. This was not going to be a centrepiece. Books were centrepieces. TVs were part of life but not to be celebrated; like going to the loo. In lower-middle-class households the salience-of-the-TV issue was coped with by way of doilies or things called 'tea towels' (dish cloths to Mum) which might be hung over the vacant but dangerous screen. But we couldn't hang things on the telly because we didn't approve of hanging things in general.

The solution was to terrify the telly, to show it all the time who was boss. Hide it; guard it, repress it, trap it with chairs and coffee tables stacked with books and magazines. Show it no mercy. Train it as you would train a dog. Only once it was obedient might it be safe.

Our first set was carried into the house by two men from Radio Rentals in overalls and gloves who might reasonably have expected that they would be plugging it in and warming it up and conducting the test all sets needed in those days while it sat in a prominent place. Like the first liberating troops marching into a previously occupied and bomb-damaged capital city, these cheery chaps were used to the warmest of welcomes, the brightest of smiles, cups of tea, as they carried black-and-white flickers of modernity into the torpid greyness of sixties Britain. In households receiving their first TV during that decade there was an element of release, of victory parade, of celebration.

Not in our home. This set went into a corner, uncomfortably jammed behind an armchair and under a bookcase. To watch it necessitated a series of manoeuvres that could not be carelessly accomplished. The TV would have to be plugged in, which required the person who had elected to watch it rather than read a book to call attention to themselves by lying on the floor and fiddling with the lead. Then the whole room – not large but already containing a table, two armchairs and that divan – would have to be reorganized so that the TV could be seen from a sedentary position. The armchairs would be manhandled into the centre of the room and then turned accusingly towards the box. I would sit on the divan behind them.*

We would watch the news. And Muggeridge. Malcolm Muggeridge was the star of my world. He was one of the big names on TV, pleasing to Mum, I think, because he was a left-wing journalist with a cut-glass accent. He was unconventional, looked down on the royal family, had a twinkle in his eye and a restless intelligence. God, it was dull, for me, at the age of ten, to have to listen to Muggeridge on Christianity, or sexual mores, or Stalin's legacy. But I thought I had to. I thought I had no choice. I thought that was what TV was. The men from Radio Rentals, bless them, made my life duller.

Except, uniquely and gloriously, by bringing me *Morecambe and Wise*, our only light entertainment. I am not sure why Eric and Ernie passed muster, but thank God

---

* Small wonder that, at the age of fifty, when the world was embracing flat-screen TVs, I bought the largest model I could afford. It takes up most of a wall. There is a sofa positioned in front of it but there isn't a corner of the room from which it is unviewable.

they did. Mum and I would watch and laugh. By the time they sang 'Bring Me Sunshine' at the end of the show we had both been transported to a better, happier, more normal place. It was joyous and frivolous. When they teased the conductor and composer André Previn and, via this piece of 1971 television magic, tweaked the tail of serious musicians and serious music, even Mother thought it funny. 'I'm playing all the right notes, but not necessarily in the right order,' Eric told Previn in their famous sketch. It became one of our catchphrases. It has brought me sunshine down the decades. I think *Morecambe and Wise* helped Mum reach an accommodation with the modern world, though even this show had its gut-wrenching moments.

In the finale to the Christmas special of 1977, a group of newsreaders came on in fancy dress, singing 'There Is Nothing Like a Dame'. This was in the days before newsreaders did anything but read the news and go home to Harpenden to mow the lawn in relative obscurity. That Christmas special was the beginning of the end of newsreader reticence. On they all trooped. Wow: they had legs. They smiled. They played the fool. And, right at the end, on came the biggest of them: Peter Woods. He had an extraordinarily low voice and delivered the last line, 'There is absolutely nothing like the frame ... of a dame', in a deep *basso profondo*.

Someone cleared their throat. My mother said: 'He had shoes the size of the *Queen Mary*.'

After a decent interval we packed the TV back in the corner. The oddness was that it wasn't odd. It was life. People with severe eating disorders sometimes report that the starvation is a form of control over lives that seem to them to be spinning out of control. You find something to cling to even if it leaves you empty. Eventually the empty feeling is itself a comfort. Repression of appetite isn't a million miles from repression of everything else. I repressed everything else.

At my interview for boarding school the headmaster asked me what I watched on television. 'Muggeridge,' I replied. I think they might have taken me out of sympathy.

All of this could be disorienting for a child trying to make sense of a world in which the truths learned at a mother's knee were far from self-evident. The campaign against the Burgesses followed a pattern but you could never quite know where the pattern led, who was truly in and truly out. At various stages of my early life there were stern edicts. Against the idea of cutting a lawn so that it had a trimmed sharp edge, against begonias (a neat little plant that lower-middle-class people, apparently, grew in their gardens), against hairdressing when it was too fussy, milk in cartons, talking about what one was eating while eating it and a host of other depravities I have either forgotten or put (halfway) out of my mind. The intensity of the outrage they could generate was sometimes more than inconvenient. At my primary school one day a master approached me as I was meeting Mum at the gate. I should have called him 'sir' but as I knew that people who said 'sir' were working class, I could not bring myself to do so. It was very awkward. He seemed more surprised than angry at my lack of manners. I doubt Mum even noticed.

And, of course, there was always the risk that some banned phrase or practice would be suddenly unbanned. Dictators create foreign enemies to foster solidarity when times are tough at home but can make peace when it suits them for reasons not available to the common folk. Mum followed that playbook to the letter. In her future, as I have mentioned, she would work for Amnesty International. What irony. Arbitrary rules imposed without appeal were her speciality. And it seemed that the rules, being unwritten, could be altered on a whim.

For instance: Granny's sweet wine. I knew this was a worry from an early age. Granny was more screwed up than Mum, I realize now. She was a properly distressed gentle-woman. Her ancestors were Protestant Irish and Austrian and didn't work. She had been brought up in Italy – why I never knew – and studied for a time at the Conservatoire in Belgium. She must have played the piano well, though I never heard her. By the time I was born pianos were not part of her life and certainly not part of mine.

She was poor. She had nothing. She lived in a rented basement flat close to us in Bath, moving in with us at the end of her life when I was away at boarding school and she could use my bedroom. When she died she left me £25 in premium bonds. Her husband, Leonard, had left her years

29

before. Granny, as I remember her in her seventies, was eccentric and fragile. And addicted – she professed with a giggle – to sweet wine, which she would decant into a medicine bottle and pour into a cup at the Wimpy Bar where, every day, she ate her lunch.

Questions arise, the principal one being: why is this not at least lower-middle class, if not actually working class? My mother had informed me before I was ten that wine was always dry. Common people drank sweet muck – Harvey's Bristol Cream sherry was a particular nose-turner – or mixed their drinks with concoctions that made them impure or easy on the palate for fear of burping and having to say pardon. But our wine was dry. It just was.

Only with Granny, it wasn't. How did one compute this? One didn't. One understood that Granny was eccentric and, for the eccentric, exceptions could be made. Granny obviously was not lower-middle class. Her soft little hands had done no work. So what was the deal? Here there is a flexibility to snobbism of Mum's kind that gives it enormous strength. Like the wings of a plane that bend and flex in turbulence, snobbism can allow itself to be buffeted but keep its shape. It can return to normal as if nothing has happened, wheels down, all bumps forgotten. Mum thought it funny when I asked about Granny and the sweet wine. 'That's just Granny,' she said. It didn't embarrass her one bit. Granny read spy novels and grew nasturtiums in a window box. She feuded with a man upstairs called Mr Packer. She drank sweet wine.

I loved Granny so much that after Mum told me who my father was, and we got the guinea pig, I told her about both events when I was alone with her one afternoon, assuming that she had not known the father information and might be interested. This was a mistake. There was a silence. It would have been working class to blab about family matters and we were not working class, she was not working class, in spite of the wine. I learned my lesson. The restraint shown by well brought-up people extended to all matters of intimacy. Exceptions were not made in any circumstances. Even in cases of obvious need. I imagine she told Mum about the conversation. Perhaps she hinted, perhaps she said outright, that it had been working class of Mum to tell me. I fear this occurred to me, somewhere deep down, though it was too damaging to be brought to the surface.

Is this also why holding hands was working class? This was another Burgess horror. On Sundays, on their way to church (oh, how I hope that's where they were going, to add retrospectively to Mum's horror), Bob and whatever his wife was called – I don't think I ever knew – would walk along their garden path and up the steps that led to the forecourt shared by our little houses, holding hands. Mum would tell me how ludicrous this was. Childish. And – a favourite word often pronounced with great fortitude – *ridiculous*.

But it was also what modern culture warriors would call a 'microaggression'. A microaggression against Mum and a very powerful one. Did Charles hold her hand? Until her son grasped her fingers in his, did anyone? Gently, soberly, tenderly? I doubt it. Class drove my mother's demons; assembled them into platoons and sent them into battle. But the demons were there already.

As I have said, I was always too polite to ask why she had married an alcoholic with a tin leg. But Mum was a sucker for charm. Stewart, the husband who had stepped on a landmine in Palestine, sounded as if he had something about him, like one of the more dissolute walk-on characters in an Evelyn Waugh satire set among the English mid-century upper classes. They had no money, Stewart and Mum, but they spent a good deal of time in pubs. I don't know how they met, or whether he joined her at the Spielplatz nudist colony, or if Petula Clark had been there, too. Mum did tell me she'd had a Vespa on which she could only make left turns, owing to her fear of the danger lurking in the middle of the road, which would need to be crossed in order to turn right. She never said anything unkind about Stewart, or Pet, or nudism, or the Vespa.

I don't know why she left her husband and that life and I never asked. But it went wrong and divorce left her alone and in need of money. Her family – still relatively well off – would not help. I don't know why but I suspect that her brother and sister saw divorce as a stain on them all. Somehow Mum ended up living in a bedsit near Sloane Square and sharing a lavatory with neighbours. I know this because she later told me she had contracted hepatitis from the loo seat. Maybe that is possible. By the time we got to talking about this part of her past life, what was very much not possible was to go into any detail without it becoming uncomfortable for her and thus for me.

There is a seediness about these early-sixties experiences that speaks of desperation. A desperation that may well have been responsible for my existence. She found a job on the *Daily Mirror*, as the newsroom secretary in the hardest of hard-bitten institutions. Fleet Street was in its pomp, money and booze flowing. Testosterone, too: the typewriters had been screwed to the desks, she recalled, because the reporters used to return from lunch drunk and throw them at each other. Having been thrust into this maelstrom, a woman who had never worked, or seen much of life, was then, just as suddenly, thrust out. The *Mirror* didn't want a single mother on the books and nor did the star reporter with whom she'd been having an affair.

Mum moved in with her mother, who had left her husband and was renting a cottage in the New Forest. She told me Peter Woods sent her a Valentine card soon after I was born and visited, awkwardly, once. Did he give her money, too? I was never quite sure, and if he did, it certainly wasn't a long-lasting arrangement. He had his own family to take care of. I think, in her heart of hearts, Mum felt he did the right thing sticking by them.

The arrival of a child requiring a secure upbringing added an urgency to the need for another marriage and another marriage was duly completed. Could it be any worse than the first? Could it hell.

The war had changed everything for her generation. Once it was over, and Mum had returned to the family home after a time spent in the country, she found the house had been occupied by Polish officers who had told Dolly the maid that she was just as good as her previous employers and should seek a life outside service. That conversation had a marked impact on Mum: it was one of the few things she ever told me about postwar Britain. She understood the logic and, in later life, the ethical force of Dolly's rebellion. Her only other war story (she was twenty-one when it ended) was about being buzzed by a flying bomb during a bus ride home, with the cockney driver grimly sticking to his route and calling out, with reference to the V2, 'Where will you 'ave it? Where will you 'ave it?' It was the accent of the driver that enthralled her, not the bomb.

I think she liked that driver. He knew his place. As I grew older, I came to realize that this 'working-class' obsession was not a blanket class war waged by Mum. She actually liked some working-class people. Genuinely liked and, in one case, loved. My playmates Alison and Rachel were joined sometimes by Emma from the flats around the corner. Emma Bamford shared a room with several siblings in a tiny flat that smelled of overcooked food. Mrs Bamford's job was to take the tickets from people who'd bought time in the Parade Gardens in the centre of the city. She looked careworn and was unquestionably working class. Mum liked her, liked Emma. They were downtrodden but cheery. They had no aspirations (that we knew of) and presented no threat. When Emma was ill once, Mum tried to lend her one of my books but was assured by Mrs Bamford that 'Emma has a book'. I suspect she merely meant that Emma had a book she was currently reading but it was glorious confirmation for Mum that this family was not in our league or seeking to be. And perhaps that was just as well.

Mum could also see the point of people who could do things. Being impractical, she valued practicality, even if she could not respect it socially. One of her closest friends was a woman called Doris Fenna, a Liverpudlian former nurse who had ended up in Bath and helped Mum with Granny when she was dying in the box-like third bedroom in our house. Doris was large and loud and entirely unfazed by Mum. She had little formal education and said what she thought. She was also immensely affectionate and immensely practical. She could deal with bodies, dead or alive. I was away at school when Granny died but in Mum's letters there was much talk of Doris being a brick, a pal, a huge help. Doris was the beginning of a better life. Peace, even atonement.

Meanwhile, there was still room for some relationships with working-class people who genuinely conformed to Mum's view of the world. In the 1970s these were still possible. In the era of the trade union – half the workforce were members of a union – the ossification of class promoted exactly the kind of caste system I have already (only a little bit unjustly) accused Mum of wanting. Forelocks were still tugged if the circumstances were right. And in our case, no circumstances were more propitious than in the relationship between Mum and the man she called 'little Den Davis'.

Little Den Davis, in his thirties, polyester shirt and slacks, neat tan shoes, slicked-back hair, ran a tiny, one-counter shop squeezed between the railway line and the road in a corner of Bath where Beau Nash never ventured. Twerton, it was called. A doctor friend in Bath tells me that Twerton is still – in a city of enormous wealth – grimly low down the national league tables for all manner of deprivation and associated risks. In the 1970s, when Bath was less wealthy and less glamorous, parts of the city were properly poor. Den's corner shop took pitiful little handfuls of coppers from the nicotine-stained fingers of pensioners by day and from ragged kids in the late afternoon. It was not much of a living but enough for a car which, with Charles persuaded by his doctors not to drive, became, from the middle of the decade, the only way I could get to and from school at the beginning and end of term.

Den, our occasional driver, was paid a pittance in cash. But so grateful. And so old-school that, before seating himself, he would hold open the door of his Vauxhall Viva for Mum to get in, closing it behind her only when she had ensured her coat was at no risk of being caught. He had no peaked cap but he drove as if he wore one. He was painfully in awe of Mum, and truth be told, of me. 'You and the other gentlemen,' he told me once, avoiding, I think on ideological grounds, the existence of girls at my school, 'are all going to make life better for us all.' At the time it seemed a stretch and in retrospect even more so. What had persuaded him that he was driving a family that was superior to him?

Well, Mum had. She was good at that, and it was still possible for even relatively distressed gentlefolk to live according to a pretence of superiority into which everyone you met just about bought.

We had a puncture once and I think the embarrassment almost killed Den when the more modern, less cowed RAC man arrived and told Mum she'd have to get out of the car while he changed the wheel. Little Den was a period piece who knew his place in our world, and Mum loved him for it.

Somewhere in the early 1970s, I fell in love with a coach driver. Harry's coach was a huge, old-fashioned beast with two wheels positioned close to each other on each side at the front. It was an assertive look that gave it an edge over other more boring vehicles with four wheels conventionally placed. Harry's coach was a machine with a soul: it needed to be coaxed up hills, squeezed carefully into spaces. It really did have a gearstick, too. Harry was a wiry little chap, not lugubrious and obese like his fellow drivers, but just as smelly. He had, as my mother pointed out, BO. On hot days he sweated and stank as he grappled with the wheel and crashed the gears. Back then, coach-driving, like so much else in life, required physical strength and effort. A man could get tired doing it. But have fun, too.

I first fell in love with Harry as I watched him shove the vehicle into gear after a refreshment break and it lurched forward over-enthusiastically. Some elderly ladies at the back squealed that they were not yet seated. 'They'll find their level,' Harry said to me with a wink.

I was in love with a working-class person but also with the delights of coach travel. This, for Mum, must have been painful. In those days our lives still revolved around the failure of the lower orders to behave properly and our efforts to live decently among them. That, of course, was the main problem: we *were* among them. We lived next door to the Burgesses.

But it was the coach trips that brought it home. Harry was employed by a company called Roman City Coaches. The most exciting day of the year was the day in February when the new brochure would come out and Mum and I went to their office in the centre of the city and picked up two copies (they were free). One was preserved as a keepsake, the other would be our guide.

Roman City would take Mum and me away for six day trips every summer – that was the rule. I would pick the longest ones because all I wanted to do was smell the smell of Harry and pretend to drive. Plymouth via Dartmoor. Swansea and the Mumbles. Brighton and Hove. Coventry Cathedral. There was not an A road in southern England that I did not traverse with Roman City.

Traverse in the company of whom? Of Harry, of course, but of Harry's other passengers, too: and this, for Mum, was the dreadful confirmation of how far she had fallen, of all that had gone wrong in her life. Family holidays with Charles were no longer manageable and nothing else was affordable. She could never escape the people she despised. All her life, until she made peace with them, they buzzed about her like flies.

Coach trips in the 1970s attracted couples in late middle age in freshly pressed fawn Crimplene jackets. Since we sat at the front, close to Harry and next to the door, and boarded first, owing to my keenness to be on the coach, we had to watch and listen as they clambered up and patted themselves down and eased their way past. Nothing we heard pleased Mum. Accents were reprehensible, observations banal. Even the roar of the engine couldn't always protect her. Famously, somewhere near Radstock, we once heard someone say, 'We've been 'ere before.' This, if you are relatively untravelled beyond Peasedown St John, is a reasonable thing for one fawn-coloured day-tripper to say to another. But for Mum it was revolting. Been here before as in a previous life? In Crimplene? If not that, then why mention it? Radstock was utterly unremarkable. How could your existence be so small, so dot-like, that you had to boast of a previous visit? She was enraged by the smallness of others, in part, at least, because their smallness illuminated hers.

In her son Mum had found an ally, or, more precisely, could set about building one. And these trips became the foundation stones of my own double life. I loved them more and more and held them in increasing contempt. Refreshment stops became opportunities to reinforce our bond, to eavesdrop on some horror phrase I could relay to Mum. To see her roll her eyes. Feel her pleasure.

I fought back only once. Mum would not eat in public. It was something only animals and working-class people did. This she decreed with one of those laughs that implied she could see the funny side of such a rule without actually seeing it at all. But on a drizzly Saturday in Teignmouth, with an hour to go before we had to get back on the coach, I suggested we both have a Mars bar. She loved it. We sat in one of those ornate Victorian beach shelters, the smells of urine and brine combining not unpleasantly around us, and ate in public.

No human bond is closer than that of a mother and son eating Mars bars in a shelter overlooking the beach in Teignmouth in the wet summer of 1973. Around us Britain was slipping into political and social despair. The IRA were blowing up stations in London. Workers were striking, the three-day week and power cuts fast approaching. Everything was falling apart. But we were cosy. I wanted to stay there for ever. In a sense I have. Part of her is still there for sure, in that shelter from the gathering storm.

On a longer and less successful visit to the north, I watched her escape from a marriage – actually say no at the altar. True, it was a manufactured affair, but it seemed hugely real at the time, and hugely consequential. She had inherited £200 from a distant relative that had enabled the two of us to go one better than our usual day trips and book a coach holiday, leaving Charles and our troubles behind. We were to go to Largs and Skelmorlie on the Firth of Clyde, just west of Glasgow. Largs and Skelmorlie! The names were so alien, so outside my known universe in the south. I had never been north of Cheltenham before but I loved maps and I knew where these places were.

Now I was to see them and spend a blissful week touring lowland Scotland courtesy of Wallace Arnold, a company that would one day supply the 'Magic Bus' on which I came close to death. This time round, Wallace Arnold looked after our physical health perfectly well, but there was a social death waiting for Mum on the road to Skelmorlie, an event as damaging as it was mundane.

It began in hitherto unimaginable joy at Bristol bus station. Diesel, for me, has always been an exciting fuel: it smells of distance, of escape. On this occasion up the M6. Up and up. The open road. So free and yet, with sickening inevitability, doomed to end in a class disaster. I really wanted this holiday to work. I wanted to like it. I wanted us to enjoy it. Yes, I winced when a 'toilet break' was announced somewhere near Lancaster but this was small stuff. I could grin at Mum and she at me and we both knew that lavatory was the word, and would always be the word, we used. In a spirit of holiday cheer, we thought little of it.

Then we arrived in Scotland and stopped at Gretna Green. And the fun began. A 'wedding' was to be arranged and the driver, quite reasonably, chose Mum, taking her, I assume, for a happy-go-lucky widow, and an actual widower from somewhere near the back of the bus. Gretna Green was all the rage at a time when marriage was still, at least in theory, a holy estate. In England you could not enter into it below the age of eighteen without your parents' consent. In Scotland you could (and can) and thousands did (and do) but this did not feel like a joyous place on a sticky day in August. It needed some jollying along. I think Mum and the unfortunate man were expected to have a mock ceremony, with some sort of fake certificate produced, and maybe to kiss, and everyone would get very excited and cheer before buying snow globes and Coke floats at the café.

Mum was genuinely upset. I was ten or so and I saw it quite clearly. This was not just an ordinary dispute among grown-ups. She created quite a scene ('How dare you!' etc.) and pulled me away from the building. We did not attend the gift shop. We got back on to the coach by forcing the door open. I was terrified that we had broken it. As usual, we had the seats behind the driver. The rest of the journey was unpleasantly tense. I imagine the driver thought she was a nutter and the other passengers thought her stand-offish. She was. But she had her reasons. I remember little of Largs except that there was a get-together in the bar of the faded, mildew-infested hotel where we were staying, and we did not go.

That holiday was the last big event before I went off to

boarding school. A house that was already silent must have become as still as a mummy's tomb. Charles was still working as an accountant in a local business so he would have been out during the day. Mum, too, had a job. She had become a secretary in a publishing company called James Brodie and Son, a family business where her social status could be subtly recognized in the privilege she enjoyed of not being required to knock on the chairman's door when she took him the letters she had opened at her desk with a delicate silver paper knife. When I visited in school holidays I noticed that they genuinely liked Mum: the family were boozy and amiable, gradually running their company into the ground, falling from whatever pedestal had once held them aloft. Spending the money, turning to seed, fading away. It was, in many ways, a good fit, at least in a family sense, with Mum's experience of postwar life.

Socially, Mum had faded, for sure, but personally she was not yet ready to give up the fight for life that had powered her through the 1960s, brought her me and Charles and left her isolated, wounded, but still kicking in the new decade. Still kicking and, to an ever-increasing degree, thinking.

Now she decided to save the world. And, as a woman always determined to side with the unconventional, she would do so in the company of the charlatans and chancers who set themselves up, in the early years of the decade, as bringers of a new order: the counterculture.

There was a book. It was called *Steal This Book* and it

was written by Abbie Hoffman, the American counterculture guru. It taught you how to rip off everything and live for free and – hilariously – it was banned in some countries in case it led to revolution. There were scams that worked in England, too, such as stealing electricity from meters and techniques for shoplifting. They were very high-minded. Contempt for what my mother called 'conventions' allowed anything to happen. Hippie life and snob life were two sides of the same coin. Neither cared for Radstock. Or people. Which was the snuggest of fits for Mum's world view.

Did Mum believe this guff in the sense of following a political programme? Of course not. She would have been most unamused if someone had stolen from us. But politics and psychology are such a mix in all of us. At various stages of our lives, in various states of distress or of comfort and quiescence, we are drawn to programmes that might give us meaning. This doesn't denude political opinions of their significance or importance: Mum had strong views and a more or less clear vision of what society should be like. She was a person of substance. But the tumult of the 1970s led many people to grasp for a political side to themselves that reflected their distress as much as anything else. 'All politics is local', the saying goes. In our home all politics was domestic.

I am not sure I was ever a natural hippie. Boys in their early teens probably never are. My clearest recollection of the lifestyle was a woman my mother became friendly with, braless and drugged up, telling me she had forgotten to take her pill and might have had sex the night before. She had frizzy hair and was massively overweight. Her forearms glistened with sweat, even in the cool of the morning. We were about to open the doors in her brass-rubbing business where, as a holiday job, I handed out the paper and cleaned the fake tombs. Joss sticks had been lit. I have been in some tight squeezes as a reporter, had some near misses, but this was properly formative. I felt violated, and not even in a way that a boy might half enjoy.

Mum's hippiedom was accompanied by a more serious and straitlaced enthusiasm for a religious sect she had read about one day in the paper. The Quakers seemed to chime with her concept of religious life: a breadth of view that allowed rather devout Jesus followers to be perfectly at ease among worshippers of not very much at all. All were linked by a seriousness of purpose and a profound sense that good ought to be done on earth to actual people or belief was not worth having. Mum was energized by the Quakers: they rescued her and she repaid the debt with fierce determination, in later life becoming an 'elder', a senior figure. A long way from tinctures with Pet Clark.

It did not end there, this one-woman renaissance. As well as being a hippie, and a Quaker, Mum became a Mao-ist. This is a heady brew. But she did it with some style, taking from each of these traditions but not entirely succumbing to any of them. She loved the hippie way because it upset people like the Burgesses but she was no fan of free love, of music not in three movements or of communal living, if it involved sharing what she would have called, with withering condescension, 'facilities'. She loved the Quakers for being sensible shoes in human form. She liked the comfort they provided but found them dull and dry. And Mao? The uniforms. She came to believe that clothes were a nuisance and a distraction and she seriously wanted a uniform imposed by the government. In the early seventies, when football hooliganism was becoming a moral panic of the age and people were talking of birching the miscreants, she had a much simpler solution: ban football. Take away their balls.

Ban schools as well. Mum became an ardent fan of a man who was a much more serious thinker than the hippies trying to steal electricity, or the high but woolly-minded opponents of nuclear weapons. The philosopher Ivan Illich wrote a book in 1971 called *Deschooling Society*. He argued that modern life, including our individual ability to think, was over-schooled. In the most famous passage of his bestselling work he rejected all of what Western modernity thought of itself as achieving:

> Medical treatment is mistaken for health care, social work for the improvement of community life, police protection for safety, military poise for national security, the rat race for productive work. Health, learning, dignity, independ-ence, and creative endeavour are defined as little more than the performance of the institutions which claim to

serve these ends, and their improvement is made to
depend on allocating more resources to the management
of hospitals, schools, and other agencies in question.

These ideas are hardly revolutionary in the modern era:
we mostly accept that the trap Illich pointed out is real and
we ought to try to avoid it. But in those days this stuff was
dynamite. For the first time in her life, free of men and the
worry about getting them and keeping them, free, most
of the time, of me, Mum was allowed her own personal
enlightenment.

A more conventional woman would have joined the
Labour Party. But snobbism plays the oddest games when
it comes to political choice. A man from the Bath branch of
the party did indeed come to the house at some point in
the early seventies. He was overweight and had a Birming-
ham accent. His name was Don. None of this was acceptable,
in particular the name: 'Don'. Mum spat it out. A single
syllable that suggested the kind of matiness she abhorred.*

My mother had no real political heroes but, if pressed,
she would probably have said that Tony Benn was her
favourite. He was left-wing but, more importantly, could
properly pronounce the things he wanted to do. No risk of
the stress in controversy straying to the second syllable, as it

* In the 1980s, while at university, I worked for Tom McNally, an MP with
a working-class background and a single-syllable first name. Mum never
met him but she knew about his enormous kindness to me and spoke of
him warmly. She was delighted when he became a peer. I think she was
over the Don thing.

did with lesser men. Furthermore, Mr Benn had renounced an hereditary peerage. He was so gently born that he could afford to ditch the title – Viscount Stansgate – in order to become an MP. What a guy. She loved Michael Foot, too; long before he was Labour leader she appreciated his bookishness. Mrs Thatcher, a fast-rising star even then, she loathed. Not because of her politics but because of her voice. The fakery of the striving classes: trying too hard, too brittle. Her pronunciation all over the shop. Her choice of reading (Frederick Forsyth) beneath contempt. If Mum and the Queen had ever had a coffee in the mid-seventies I imagine they'd have been rolling their eyes together at the prospect of a Thatcher ascendancy.

We were superior. We were above the worldly battles. Yet all too often Mum's desire to be different, to throw off shackles, real or imagined, led her into behaviour that seems, in retrospect, unhinged.

For instance: the new version of Mum was extremely keen that I took up smoking, and during one of our day trips, I did. We bought matches and cut some bracken-like plant by the side of the road – the dead tubes of the stems made cigars that burned for minutes. Acrid smoke, slightly sweet, poured out. I did not inhale, thank God, but we took some of these stems home and that year I smoked them in my room, filling it with pungent clouds and giving myself immense, unstoppable headaches. Once I was sick – suddenly and violently – out of my window over the back garden. It was cleared up without anything being said.

In the summer of 1975 I came home from school for the holidays to find eight cannabis plants growing in the sitting room. We had a big, metal-framed picture window that caught the morning sun. I pretended I was pleased and she treated it in the same way she had treated our talk about sex a year or so earlier: 'Do you know about all this stuff? Good.'

The plants yielded a crop of nice-smelling leaves which we dried and, somewhere along the way, lost. My mother would never have smoked anything. But cannabis was completely illegal then and this was, to be frank, a deeply irresponsible thing to do.

She also gave me a 'Legalize Cannabis' T-shirt. It was bright yellow with green lettering. What was she thinking?

These days we would talk of breakdowns and low-level depression. I remember teasing her when she started taking pills called Quiet Life. We already had a quiet life. The quietness was the problem, or part of it. The pills were unlikely to unlock any massive improvement in our general situation but she took them anyway, washed down with Gold Blend.

A couple of years before the cannabis incident, there had been another change, which I think was brought on by contemplation of our general situation. A record-player for me: a wooden mono box, with a control for volume and for tone, bought in a junk shop. This was an important moment as it would introduce sound into a home that, until now, had heard mostly only Bach, and mostly in the early morning. And then, during the day, nothing. Deep silence penetrated all of life and followed us out of our home. Quiet Life indeed. The silence was profound and the shock of the noise of the outside world could be destabilizing.

Once, in the middle of the night, the phone rang. Telephones in those days were in halls and took years to have installed. Having been installed – and I don't think this was peculiar to our house – they were treated with some suspicion. They were expensive to use and often, when they rang, the news they brought had to be grim to warrant the cost. 'Bath 60476?' I would hear Mum say, as in, why are you ringing? What could this be about? The phone was not intended to be used at night. It was not designed for out-of-hours trivialities.

Now, at three in the morning, it was ringing. The house was exploding with sound. Noise, which Mum abhorred. Which brought on her headaches. Stomach-twisting panic. Voices – at three in the morning! Mum and Charles both stumbling out of rooms. I can't remember who answered. The call was from one of Charles's children by his first marriage. They'd been in America and got the time wrong. Soon they were gone. But the phone call in the night was unforgivable. It was Hades come to Wells Road. The intensity of our lives accentuated the tiniest deviation from the norm into a catastrophe. We could not cope with errant phone calls. We could not cope with the sounds and smells of ordinary life. It was all so fragile. If we were quiet, if we were haughtily polite, if we were 'sensible', we could find a way through. True, I suppose, we did. But a life so disturbed by a phone call in the night is a life lacking in resilience, and a life lacking in resilience is a life lacking in the joy that resilience brings.

It was a life into which music was about to be introduced but not lightly, not easily, not frivolously. Music had always been a class issue of the very tickliest variety. I had been allowed to have a record collection which, on occasions when silence was deemed unnecessary, I was permitted to use on the gramophone in the sitting room. But having music on in the background while doing something else was unacceptable. It was the behaviour of the building site.

My first purchase was '20th Century Boy' by T. Rex. We sat listening, Mum and I, as Marc Bolan sang:

> I'm like a car, I drive like a plane
> I wanna hang your head in the falling rain.

Neither Mum nor I had the foggiest idea what was happening here. We tried getting long-play records from the library (LPs were too expensive to buy) and ended up with Janis Joplin's posthumously released *Pearl*. We listened to the track entitled 'Cry Baby'. 'Quite orgasmic,' Mum said. A long silence descended.

She tried another tack. Out of the blue a more acceptable LP was bought. We made a special trip to a cavernous shop full of bearded men and women with grey ponytails leafing through sheet music. Duck Son & Pinker was an institution in posh Bath throughout my childhood, though that was the first and only time I crossed its threshold. It had opened in 1848, catering to the folk who built the smart parts of the city, and then, in the 1960s and 1970s, to the Bath Festival set – people who knew not to clap between movements. Mum's people. I think we can be certain that none of them had ever been on a coach trip. Alongside the sheet music were records: Deutsche Grammophon classical music. A selection was made: Shostakovich's Piano Concerto No. 2. There was a drum in the first movement, Mum explained. And the kind of rhythm that she detected I might like, on account of my previous inferior music choices.

We sat and listened. I tried to be middle class that afternoon harder than I had ever tried before. But nothing came with the drums and cheery tinkling. On and on it went. We sat opposite each other in big fawn armchairs with antimacassars on the arms for ease of washing. Our heads swayed slightly (which was allowed), but there was no talking over the tune (not allowed) and no reducing the length of time it took to get to the end of the first movement.

Which finally arrived. The drums were quiet. The second movement, the andante, was about to come on. 'Shall we try it?' I hesitated. Why not? Mum had picked up the *Guardian*. This did not seem to be a success.

The second movement of Shostakovich's second piano concerto is without question one of the most affecting pieces of music known to man. Play it to a child growing up in strange circumstances and you will allow him to see – to hear – the depths of his despair. Stringed instruments soar, in what I now know to be a minor key, and the piano is brought in after what seems like an age of waiting to play (in a major key, quiet but insistent) the truest, the saddest tune I had ever heard. It's occasionally jaunty. Sometimes brittle. Then slow and unsure. It loses its way. Does it find it? By the end I wanted to put my arms around the record-player, to be inside it. Sometimes I still cry when I hear this music.

'A bit sissy' was Mum's take. To avoid awkwardness, I agreed.

I preferred Slade, I said. But now that I had my own record-player, I could combine 'Cum On Feel the Noize' with Shostakovich. I could sit and listen on my own. I could contemplate what was going wrong. I could plot rebellion. No, not rebellion. Too extreme. And I had nowhere to go. But with every passing day of my mid-teens it was becoming clear that Mum was not always the force for good that she suggested she was. This was not her fault, of course. She would never have consciously done anything that reduced an iota of my life chances. But she couldn't help herself. She had created a vortex as much as a relationship. I loved her more and more and it helped me less and less.

In the wider world Mum thought two big changes were going to come. The first was an end to the torture of

prisoners of conscience and the second was the abandonment of all nuclear weapons. Both were being directed, it
seemed to me, from the basement of the Friends' Meeting
House in the centre of Bath. Mum took up with great
enthusiasm these twin causes of peace and was determined to be at the forefront of both. It helped, I think, that
both were almost entirely the preserve of the middle
classes. Our weekly meetings with Amnesty International
letter-writers brought us into contact with earnest people
in tie-dye dresses using their considerable literary skills
to persuade prison wardens in far-off lands that prisoner
X or Y was not guilty of any real crime and was much
admired in Georgian Bath. CND night was a little more
politically charged but essentially the same people attended.
Afterwards we would sometimes go back to their flats,
where they would smoke weed. Hessian wallpaper was
a thing.

Why do people believe what they do about politics and
justice? Although I automatically thought of myself through
my early teens as left-wing, a radical, a peacenik, actually
something else was afoot.

This was a flowering time in my mother's life. She had
discovered not who she was but who she had decided to be.
To the books of Ivan Illich and the 'Small is Beautiful' econ-
omist E. F. Schumacher she added deep friendships with
serious campaigners. Might it have led to some kind of
added satisfaction for her outside the home, as it were? The
answer was a pretty firm no. Mum had a view of sex that

can best be described as toxic. Toxic femininity. Mum's marriage was hopeless but there was something that prevented her from achieving any kind of companionship with anyone except me. Toxic femininity ruled our home and probably damaged her and me. Toxic in the sense that it saw men as rapacious and dangerous and yet desired nothing more than to be seduced by them. I remember an early chat about relationships in which Mum said boys should have lots of girlfriends 'to see what they liked', but girls could easily become 'used'. It was Victorian. Girls (including her) must be both chaste and chased. Chaps, on the other hand, were always sinners, oglers, users, leavers.

The only man in Bath I ever felt she was close to was spectacularly unsuitable. He had a military past – SAS, at least in the telling – and was huge with a shaven head and tree-trunk arms. He told me once he had been hit by a car but walked home fine: the car had been written off. I was impressed: but seriously, Mum? He had come to an Amnesty International evening and for a few months his was one of the flats we visited. I don't think Mum ever went without me and after a while he disappeared from the scene.

And that really was it. She had given birth at thirty-six to a child the father didn't want and had found no lasting attachment since then. Had she known love? I doubt it. The end of the war had brought a kind of mad mating scramble. Apart from the man who died on the train (or soon after getting off it), there had been one who had taken her to the Ritz in the middle of the night and ordered a boiled egg. This was a story she told often: it was about how life was properly lived alongside institutions that could be trusted to recognize quality and adapt instantly to its demands. The glamour of the Ritz was not interesting – it was all about the egg. And the power. The impassive faces of the waiting staff. 'Of course, sir. Hard-boiled or soft?'*

Another man – Mum revealed no details about him – once suggested that they attend a course in economics together. My mother was utterly and proudly innumerate and had no interest in economics. On this course, Mum told me, she had learned only one thing: that man's desires are unlimited. How we laughed.

When it came to the desires of the little man she was

---

* In 2016 I was passing the Ritz on Piccadilly when I noticed the top but-ton had come off my shirt. I was giving a talk to some business people in an office nearby and I needed to look my smartest. Did I dare? I did. Mum had died a decade before but I paid homage to her and to the story of the boiled egg. I strode, as she would have strode, through that same quietly grand door and looked, as she would have looked, as if I needed some help and expected to get it. I asked if someone might sew the button back on. Without a scintilla of hesitation, I was ushered into a side room where the mending was done with enormous enthusiasm and not the slightest hint of a question about why I should expect, as a random man off the street, this kind of assistance.

As I was leaving I got cocky. I approached the doorman and asked for a taxi. 'Of course, Mr Vine. Have a wonderful day.'

They had let me in and fixed my shirt because they thought I was my fellow broadcaster Jeremy Vine, whose fame had spread with his appear-ance the previous year on *Strictly Come Dancing*. It was not good breeding that had won the day but mistaken identity and celebrity. Mum would have rolled her eyes. She is better off out of the modern world.

bringing up, the whole thing was slightly more complicated. Mum was hugely keen that I made it in the world
but just as keen that the bond between us should not be
broken. She wanted me to make it in her world.

She was always in charge: she even policed grief. There
are two funerals I should have gone to. The first was for my
Uncle Oliver's wife Ann. The second was for Granny. I
loved both of them and both had loved me. Was that why
I wasn't invited?

Ann was a little too good to be true. Central casting
would have been embarrassed to have provided her. An
army wife. Given to talk about 'knockers' and 'arses'. Tick.
Huge smile, loud voice. Big ticks. Devotion to duty, oh yes.
My uncle, my mother's younger brother, had chosen a
woman as jolly and open as he was sour and closed. Oliver
was an officer in the Royal Artillery. He'd lost a finger in a
gunnery accident in Korea. Major Crocombe was then
persuaded by an older friend in military intelligence to try
to learn Arabic and found he had a talent. He became a
spy, then an arms-dealer, and ended up doing God knows
what for the Sultan of Oman. All the time Ann had giggled
along at his side. They had come back to live near Bridg-
water in Somerset, where he set up a business teaching
people to drive. Was it a front? Le Carré would have
thought it barely plausible. Whatever the reason they were
there, poor Ann was as happy in the village of Enmore as
she had been in Oman and Tripoli and Baghdad, until the
day she filled a bath with hot water while Oliver went

shopping for groceries and, after suffering an epileptic fit, drowned.

'Water made a damned mess,' Oliver told Mum. Which roughly translated as: 'I loved her and will never find happiness with anyone else.'

I wrote him, on Mum's advice, a letter of condolence. He wrote back by return of post thanking me stiffly and mentioning that he had changed his will. Her funeral would have been a desperately sad affair. They had no children but her parents were still alive and she was much loved by all those in the family who found Oliver strange. But I was not part of it. Too difficult to arrange.

As it had been with Granny. Dear Granny, mourned properly by no one but me, the grandchild she had seen every day when I was young and she was old. Granny, whose ashes were briefly kept on our mantelpiece in Wells Road before being lost. Mum told me she had picked them up from the crematorium and brought them back on the bus, which I think she saw as short-story-worthy pathos but actually was not necessary. She could have performed these tasks with others if she had chosen. Mum rejected society, turned her nose up at convention. But funerals are a convention with a purpose. They have stayed in fashion for good reason.

Of course, at funerals, people cry. I might have. She might have. And this would never have done. The repression of emotions came easily to my mum's whole generation – there is nothing unique about her here – but in the distilled atmosphere of our home repression became a habit that turned into a vortex. More and more questions to pose, but fewer and fewer actually posed. True, in decades gone by children were less involved in all manner of activities and life events, including funerals. Death was still a shame, to be endured behind closed doors. An unmentioned thing. But these funerals were central to my life. Why didn't I ask about Granny's funeral? Why did I not demand that I should be there? I don't know.

But of course I know.

3

Garage Doors

She hit him. Not just once. I see her shouting some more, turning away, then coming back: whack, on the side of his head. Not neatly, as in a film. Catching his ear; a dull sound, a thud, not a ringing slap.

We are in a room in a guest house at Croyde Bay, North Devon. It's a holiday, in the days when we still had 'family' holidays. Suitcases. Sun lotion. Meals out. Meals together: they are the worst moments, as all dysfunctional families know. Nuclear family holidays have a narrative weight. They are freighted with meaning. They can be happy or less happy but if they are not 'normal', all the panic buttons flash. Ignore the flashing lights and the pressure builds up until, by the beach, when things are still not as they should be, the tension between what is and what should be becomes too much for physics to bear. It's like those foolish *Doctor Who* plots where a tear is made in the known universe and all of reality is sucked through it.

That holiday had begun with customary stress. Long before the car journey came the preparation for the car journey. Any travel of more than a few miles required, from Charles, meticulous, crazed research and pre-planning. He would need to find his leather driving gloves. An Ordnance Survey map of the area being targeted would be brought out from the collection of maps that would itself have to be retrieved from the attic. It would be unfolded and checked for wear. Could you still see the symbols? A church without a spire in Hatch Beauchamp; a disused railway line near Shepton Mallet; the red lines, the A roads which, in the pre-motorway days, were the uncertain arteries of Britain.

Sometimes, in the folds of the map, things would become indistinct. Charles could not bear the thought of being off the map for even half an inch of cloth and paper mix. A trip into Bath would be required to a specialist map shop full of chaps planning things. Then, a week or more before D-day, the tyres would be attended to. Fluids would have to be added to the car and then monitored – were their levels remaining constant or dropping off again? Would the oil last? In the event of getting stuck behind a tractor spewing silage from its back wheels, would the washer fluid hold out? A day or two before departure, the Hillman would be reversed out of the garage and polished until it glowed.

On the allotted date, at around 3.30am, the night still

fully dark, alarms would go off, eviscerating our preter-natural silence, and a deeply unpleasant start made to the process of travelling for fun. Mum and Charles would pack the bags that had been ready for days into the car. Food and water would be stowed for the journey. And then we were off and the achievement noted (by them both) that they had 'missed the crowds'.

Ah yes, we missed the crowds. We were seldom around when other people were around. That would have been bad: for us and for them. We tore through the early dawn light in that foolish little car. I longed to open the window in the summer; for playful breezes. Charles would not allow open windows for fear of his hair being ruffled. He could stand no interference with his personal space, not even from the breeze. Perhaps he felt it was teasing him. So the Hillman was as sealed as it was possible for a 1970s car to be.

I doubt it took as long as three hours to get to Croyde Bay in the summer of 1970 and yet the first, deeply disap-pointing, thing we did on arrival was to rest. It was mandatory. Charles decreed that, as the driver, he would require silence and sleep. Mum was bound to keep to this rule because she had not driven and could not drive. We had three beds in a room with a sink and we had to lie on them. I read *Knights of the Cardboard Castle* by Elisabeth Beresford, a tale of upper-middle-class children repelling louts who want to destroy their pretend castle. There's a salt-of-the-earth character, of whom Mum would have approved, a working-class man – a caretaker or handyman,

I think, who helps the gentle children win their battle. I wanted to disappear into it.

But reality was Croyde Bay. Our hotel was Fawlty Towers in all but name. Only less genteel. On that first evening after dinner an invitation reached us: to gather in the bar and sing. For their different reasons it was clearly highly unlikely that either Mum or Charles would take part. For me: panic. I wanted this holiday to go well. As I always wanted everything to go well. The sheet of paper under the door ('Come and join in the sing-song until late!') was one of those frequent events in my early life which spoke of imminent disaster.

It rumbled, the row.

'Why are we in this place?'

'Who booked it?'

'We have to leave.'

'We can't leave.'

'We should go home.'

'The boy . . .'

Then the singing began.

One of the features of the hotel for me had been the rather grand landing outside our room. It had faded brown paint, a purple carpet stained with ancient wine, dropped or thrown, and a cracked chandelier connected to the high ceiling by a long metal pipe. It was shabby but it was large, draughty, lived-in. Our landing at home was too small to allow two people to pass each other. Our paint was unchipped because our home saw little action. It was exciting to see how life could affect a building.

But it was also echoey. Very. The sounds of merriment were conducted right up the stairs and, it seemed, funnelled right into our room.

It was not late, perhaps nine o'clock. Charles was in a dressing gown with a silk tassel. He had staring eyes and a beard. He looked utterly crazy. He was. He announced that he would go downstairs and demand that they were quiet. That word 'quiet' really struck me. Even at the age of nine, and having seen little of the world, I sensed it was unlikely that just being quieter would be enough, and that in any case this request had little chance of being successful. I very seldom admired Charles, still less ever wanted to emulate him. But that evening I think I felt that he was somehow engaged in something rather glorious – the closest North Devon ever got to the charge of the Light Brigade. It felt valiant as well as disastrous, even before he marched on to the landing.

There was indeed silence. For a few moments. Then they laughed at him. Someone told him to eff off. The piano started again. He came upstairs. He was out of ideas and Mum was out of patience. He stood by the mirror. I was behind them, on my bed. I am not sure why she hit him. It is possible that he hit out first. It is, as these things so often are, a blur. A blur with fine detail intermingled. He had a comb, and after each blow he would re-comb his hair, holding one side down while vigorously attending to the other. The terror I felt was that this was the beginning of a chain of events that would lead to her being damaged, to us being damaged, to the end of everything.

The singing eventually stopped. We must have slept. We probably went to the beach. I cannot remember whether the holiday was cut short but our journey home was uneventful. In *Knights of the Cardboard Castle* everything is resolved and the children, all manner of scrapes left behind them, go home to bed. I was aware, dimly, of how things should be.

Eventually I discovered the answer to that question I used to ask when I was young: 'Where did we get Charles?' I genuinely don't think Mum ever answered it directly but at some stage in my teens the riddle was solved. Perhaps a cousin told me. Or maybe my Aunt Charmion, on one of the days when she had found my mother too priggish to be bothered with. The answer was that she had found him in the *New Statesman*. Charles had advertised for a housekeeper, and responded kindly when Mum suggested she could do the job but had a young child. She had been living with her own mother in a house in the New Forest, suitably out of the way for an unmarried mother in 1961. It was time to break free. Charles provided the opportunity. I am not sure who came out worse from the deal. I have no idea how their relationship began or how it ended in marriage. There are no photos of the wedding.

Charles had worked for the Bank of England in London.

He would have been a clerk in a junior position but still quite a fancy job for a man whose parents were shopkeepers in the Home Counties. But something had gone wrong. He had been unable to cope. He moved to Bruton and ran the post office in what was then a sleepy Somerset village, long before it became a nirvana of second homes and quinoa salad. Charles was washed up there. Hidden, or hiding, among the farmers. This is all I ever knew. Except that there had been a previous marriage and children, older than me, about whom I was not encouraged to ask. Crucially, he had enough money for a house. And for years after he was gone Mum received a small Bank of England pension. He was a shelter from the storm. A shelter, but leaky.

Too leaky? It must have seemed touch and go. Her head, on the bus home from the doctor's office on the day she received the diagnosis of madness for her new husband, would have been filled with the newly revealed complexities of an already not straightforward life. I can see the route, along a moderately fast road, the bus picking up speed as it carried her into her post-diagnosis life, via a detour into the neatest of postwar estates. Solid houses too far from the centre of Bath to be highly prized but still of the city. Lots of belonging and certainty in Combe Down, the area I am thinking of. A fire station with a tower on which they could practise rescues. Little groups of shops, set back from the road, a pet store, a newsagent, a cheap hairdresser. In those days no cafés, but maybe a local butcher. People making for home, making for the bus. Lives troubled, as lives are, but normal, as lives can be, too. She must have scanned it all as she went home. Perhaps she toyed with the idea of leaving.

But she stayed. It was one of those *Sliding Doors* decisions that life brings. In the 1998 film with Gwyneth Paltrow, we get to see two different plots unfolding from a moment when a tube train was either narrowly missed or narrowly caught. We don't, in my life, get to see the non-Charles version.

So we are stuck with the reality Mum was stuck with. The reality of madness. Which is a reality based not – as it is so often in films – on dramatic moments of transcendental dottiness resulting in denouements and resolutions. Still less on that other lazy film motif where mental illness automatically leads to violence against family or strangers. In *Joker*, from 2019, for example, Joaquin Phoenix's character Arthur stops his medication and becomes ever more violent. Which encourages the view that this outcome is true. It isn't.

The reality, the broad reality but also my reality, our reality at 90 Wells Road, Bath, was so much more mundane. And yet, in its mundanity, just as difficult to cope with. As good a place as any to start is in the garage.

We have to go inside. Where no violence was ever done. No one foamed at the mouth or had to be restrained. But still terrible things happened here. Tortures were inflicted. A life unravelled in the tight space around the Hillman, between the boxes where the padlocks were kept, dead weight upon dead weight.

Charles's illness began with what would now be called a

personality disorder. He could not accept that anything anyone ever said or did in front of him, or to him, was anything other than part of a plot. The term 'persecution complex' is too strong: he seemed to believe that many of the slights aimed at him were glancing blows and he could laugh them off. But every day, in every way, the slights kept coming. They would lead, in the early years, to intense discussions about ordinary domestic affairs. Perhaps these were normal? Children don't know. For instance: it was decided that two copies of the *Guardian* should be delivered every day because someone somewhere was suggesting that Charles was not a free thinker. That word 'free' was part of the row that led to the ordering of the extra paper. 'I am not a yes man!' Charles roared.

When it got really bad, in our house of silence he would deploy noise. Not any old noise, it was true – sublime noise to some. But over-amplified to a degree that made the walls of our little box reverberate and the neighbours complain. With no hope of being heard. The record-player would be employed to drown out the voices, human and otherwise, real and imagined, that caused him so much upset. And, as I have recounted, it was always Bach. The obvious violin pieces but also the harpsichord concertos. Someone once called them 'sewing-machine music' and the description is perfect: a kind of rhythmical whirring with little tweets, flittery-jittery tunes.

He would sit in the armchair next to the record-player, motionless. After rows, but sometimes, too, in the early morning at first light, to ward off something or someone. Bach was his real companion. A composer who was disciplined, methodical, ordered, reaching across the centuries to touch a troubled mind. At the end of the last movement the mechanical arm would take the stylus off the disc and return it to its holder. And silence would return.

But Bach could not reach the garage. And something was happening there. To be exact: people were getting in and altering things, 'to show who's boss'. It's another phrase that echoes down my childhood and through poor Charles's life. It was the subtlety of their approach that tortured him so much. They would enter at night and slightly move the windscreen-wipers on the Hillman. They would reduce the oil level. Occasionally they would wind down the driver's-door window – just the teeniest bit – in order to make their mark. It was daily, this sinister, assiduous work being carried out in the garage, and it drove him madder and madder. And Mum, too. And me.

The necessary resistance became a vast, ongoing project in which the doors, the thin metal up-and-under type favoured on housing estates since the 1960s, had to be replaced regularly. And then, when that seemed to Charles to be failing, replaced with an entirely new design. We had, as I remember, a succession of barn-door replicas, built to fit the garage at great cost by bemused specialist manufacturers. One was about five inches thick. I could not open it alone.

Big doors don't come cheap. My mother would remonstrate about the needless expense. She would point out the pointlessness of it. They would argue. Money got very tight. The children who lived near us would come round less frequently and never stay for tea. Charles was becoming eccentric to the point of being frightening. I imagine their parents told them to stay away. Silences would descend on the house and last for days.

There was a birthday that brought things to a head, if only briefly and temporarily. A small fruit cake was provided. We sat down, the three of us. I served myself and ate a chunk. Charles, sternly but not unreasonably, instructed me that cake was to be shared. I remember a pause before my mother screamed at him: 'How the fuck is he supposed to know that in this fucked-up house, when no one ever comes here?' I was probably eight and remember thinking, 'She's right, they don't.' Until that moment, I hadn't actually thought through the oddness of our lives. It was there in the background. That day, via that unusual blow-up, it was in the foreground. Was that any better? If there is nothing you can do about something, maybe keeping it in the background is best. Bach played long into that January night.

Some nights Charles would sleep in the garage, in pyjamas and dressing gown, the cord tightly knotted. I would see him trudge up the steps to the forecourt in front of our house. I would hear him come in at first light. One Christmas he decided, in the middle of the night, to drive off somewhere. The driveway from the forecourt to the road was a steep 30-yard hill. It had been snowing and we woke (everyone in the neighbourhood woke) to the sickening sound of the car wheels rotating crazily on ice and gravel. He was completely stuck. Again and again he tried to make it up the hill. Again and again he failed. Net curtains twitched. At first light I saw a neighbour emerge with some sacking, perhaps thinking that Charles's mission was urgent and it might be the wisest course of action to facilitate it. The sacking did not help and Charles left the car at the bottom of the hill, the slamming of the door echoing, it seemed to me, around the whole city. Bach's harpsichord music accompanied the early light that would see us emerge, bleary-eyed and shell-shocked, into Boxing Day.

Then there were the driving lessons. What possessed them? I suppose it was Mum's desperation. We had had a couple of serious near misses with Charles at the wheel. She told friends (as they later told me) that she needed to protect us. She needed to be able to take over. It must have been 1972 when she decided that the moment had come for her to start to drive. I was eleven and had an awareness of danger. God knows, they didn't. Each 'lesson' built on the last. In that each was worse. On the first, Charles took us up one of the hills outside the posh parts of the city. They swapped places and he instructed Mum in the mechanics of driving while I sat in the back. There were no seatbelts. I had brought a book. I think Mum – who could be staggeringly unworldly – had thought getting the hang of it would take ten minutes, after which we might tour smoothly around the West Country and return home for tea.

She could not start the engine. Then, when it was started,

she could not manage the clutch, and the car stalled with a sickening jump. The world's worst driver was teaching the world's worst pupil and they couldn't stand each other even before the engine turned. Lesson two, a week or so later, saw her manage the ignition OK but we still didn't get anywhere. Lesson three, on a Sunday to reduce traffic interference, was the last one. I can still see, in slow motion, the horror unfold. Mum was moving in second gear but someone was overtaking and she was panicked. She decided to turn off the road and, remembering to follow Charles's strict advice that all manoeuvres should be preceded by use of the indicator, she flicked at the stick. It came off. I can see it now, arcing through the air, head over tip over head over tip, and landing in his lap. By this time, she had made her turn and we were careering into a field, where the car came to rest.

There was a good deal of shouting. She cried, which I had never seen before. Someone stopped, thinking this might be a serious accident, and she and I took the offer of a lift home. I remember a big saloon car with a friendly, gentle driver who kept to one side of the road, drove easily with one hand, chatted about the weather. He had a radio tuned to Radio 2. How things should be.

Did Charles and I have any moments together, just us two? Only a few. He once took me to see Portsmouth play Bristol City. We sat in the smart bit of the ground (football grounds in those days were mostly standing) and watched in silence. It had been a surprise gift, this trip, and halfway through he asked me if I was, indeed, surprised, and I said yes. And that was that. He could think of nothing to say to a young boy he would have sensed (known, perhaps) was being groomed to loathe him. And the boy had nothing to say, either. So we went to the football together and went home together but resolved nothing. If those people Charles thought monitored his every move had really been watching they would have witnessed a bleak Saturday scene: a goalless draw.

Mum would have raised her eyes.

How different life could have been if I had been freer. Different for me but different for him, too. Mum arranged the way things were in our home and Mum did for Charles. He was, as Dr Neil had put it in that brutal encounter soon after their marriage, completely mad. But he was also completely human. There was some violence – as I have said, in both directions, I think – but never any towards me. I was frightened of him, frightened of all men, owing to that vague Mum-induced sense that they were capable of doing terrible things, though based on no proper reasoning. Could he have been a normal stepfather? No, but he could have been given the chance to try.

Larkin should have written, 'They groom you up, your mum and dad'. It would have been less effective, I suppose, but truer. Mum had taken a decision (before or after the madness diagnosis, who knows?) that Charles and I were to be separate. The oddness of him was accentuated, encouraged even. We were not to be close even by accident, even if, on occasion, it might have helped us both.

She was diligent in keeping him away from anything or anyone she cared about. My cousin Gregory Woods is a poet. Gregory is a little older than me and remembers being encouraged to read poetry by Charles and to listen to music. On a visit to our home Gregory sat in our sitting room and listened to a string quartet with this strange and intense, unsmiling man. It was not a punishment (though it may have felt like one) but an honest, if plodding, effort to introduce a youngster to chamber music, and thus assist him in becoming civilized. Mum had put her head round the door and scolded her husband, 'Leave him alone, he doesn't care about Mozart.'

But what I now know is that Charles persisted. If anything, aiming at an even higher level of highbrow. Later that year he sent Gregory a book. It was the Chilean communist Pablo Neruda's *Twenty Love Poems and a Song of Despair*.

Every day you play with the light of the universe.
Subtle visitor, you arrive in the flower and the water.
You are more than this white head that I hold tightly
as a cluster of fruit, every day, between my hands.

You are like nobody since I love you.
Let me spread you out among yellow garlands.
Who writes your name in letters of smoke among the stars
   of the south?
Oh let me remember you as you were before you existed.

Gregory was probably nineteen. This was a stretch. But it worked. My cousin still has the book. It was one of the reasons he became a poet. Behind the ever-changing garage doors, in moments when the voices were calm, Charles must have been a man capable of understanding profound truths, intuitions about love and lust that didn't really penetrate our home, and, if the gift is anything to go by, he understood the importance of communicating those things. Charles himself owned few books and often what he read was designed to show some imaginary watcher that he was not going to be cowed or bullied. But he did have books of poetry. Including a collection in which I found, as I leafed through it one day in my early teens, Stevie Smith's 'Not Waving But Drowning'.

> Oh, no no no, it was too cold always
> (Still the dead one lay moaning)
> I was much too far out all my life
> And not waving but drowning.

It should have been an epiphany. It could have been. Charles and I could have talked about it. The poem is famous because it is as approachable as it is disturbing. It is about a misunderstanding, to put it mildly. The kind of misunderstanding that our life in Wells Road was built around. But 'too far out' means what it says. There isn't a way back. I suppose that's the point, isn't it?

We were not poor but we were tense. Money was not

easy. Charles earned enough for us to live on and I don't think there was much of a mortgage on our little box. But there was no leeway, either. Every Sunday, Mum and Charles would sit in the kitchen and she would account for the money she had spent on housekeeping and receive a thing called an allowance. The 1970s were trying so hard to look modern, to be modern, but they were still the 1970s. In homes around the country, things that would not have been out of place in 1924, the year Mum was born, were still carrying on. Some of them deeply unpleasant, particularly for women. This was one of the milder pieces of baggage from the past. Mum was allowed to spend a certain amount a week on Quiet Life tablets or lunches with me in the Wimpy Bar. If she went over, there would be questions and a reckoning.

How could this be? Was she not outraged by this 'conventional' stuff? Not really. I don't think she ever really questioned it. For all her abandonment of other conventions, for all her modernity in so many areas of life, this was what she knew. Her own father had probably done it. She was a supplicant and he the provider. Perhaps she knew, deep down, for all that she disparaged him, that Charles had this function and should be able to exercise the power that went with it.

She also had to contend, as I suggested at the start, with a world that regarded mental health as a private matter, and often a shameful matter. It was giggled at on the TV and hinted at in public but suffered in private, in families, or what was left of them. This was a world in which, in children, the official term 'subnormal' had recently been replaced by 'backward': and this was considered progress.

Mum never talked to me about mental health. She would not have had the vocabulary. I am not sure the vocabulary really existed then. But she had on her shelves a book that I used to flick through with horrified fascination, a book I later learned was a classic. And a window into a life that Charles had escaped, just. Anyone with a child with learning difficulties will tell you that coping in the 2020s can be tough but the distance we have travelled since the 1970s is staggering.

The book was called *The Empty Hours*. It was published in 1971 and its author, Maureen Oswin, had, I subsequently discovered, changed Britain.

It was horrifying. It spoke of a world of unrelenting pain at a time when people with mental illness and people with neurological conditions were lumped together and kept apart from everyone else. I would have been reading it at the age of eleven or so, too young to understand more than the gist of what it revealed, but an advanced enough reader to realize that this was ghastly. Thousands of children suffered appalling abuse, often sleeping on mattresses in cockroach-infested dormitories, far from their families. They were tranquillized and left to a life of endless, formless, listless hopelessness. The empty hours of the title were the weekends when, in many of these institutions, nothing at all happened. I read the accounts in secret, with a sickly sense that they somehow impinged on our home, and yet didn't. I never knew why Mum had this book but I suspect she wondered about how Charles's life might have turned out if his mental health had fallen apart earlier.

And although the asylums for children were awful, even worse, in many ways, were the places where the adults could end up. We were still a nation that locked up the mentally ill as a matter of course. Loony bins, they called them. Mum made no pretence of liking Charles or wanting him around but she could have had him committed to one of these dreadful institutions. She could have been free. Instead she stuck with him. Stuck at it. Coping, daily, with a man teetering on the brink of madness. Did her reading of the Maureen Oswin book change his fate? It is possible. As I turned the pages, I imagined myself in an asylum and shivered with the pleasure of knowing that I was not. Not quite.

Charles was also capable of being loved, if not by us. His children by his first marriage would stay in sporadic contact and in later life they would visit. I am not sure they were always given the welcome they deserved. There was a coldness in the way Mum treated them; a distance that spoke of more than just separate families. She talked to me of them as if they were aliens. The only thing I remember hearing was that they were all failures – in love, in careers, in life generally. I am not even sure they were. But they were part of Charles, they were of him. Human cruelty begins at home. Including some of the psychological wellsprings of conflict and misery. Entire wars and purges can begin with the process of 'othering' a particular group; we are, in a crowd or an ethnic category or a religious affiliation, deeply persuadable that we are better, more human, more worthy of fulfilment, than whichever segment of humanity we decide to 'other'. Then we can hate them with impunity. Our consciences are clear because they brought this on themselves.

This can happen at home. And Mum knew it. In her later years she read Simone de Beauvoir's *The Second Sex*. I saw it on her shelves. She may have been familiar with this passage:

> Thus humanity is male and man defines woman not in
> herself but as relative to him; she is not regarded as an
> autonomous being . . . She is defined and differentiated
> with reference to man and not he with reference to her; she
> is the incidental, the inessential as opposed to the essential.
> He is the Subject, he is the Absolute – she is the Other.

When I read it, long afterwards, I thought immediately of Charles. Simone de Beauvoir was making a gender point – and one that needed to be made – but her description of the male–female dynamic applied equally in our household in the other direction. I am sure Mum was fully trapped in the deepest of gender roles and unconscious societal biases but in our home the traps were laid, and fallen into, by the males. Charles was the incidental, the inessential as opposed to the essential. The other. This was how our household worked. It was not deliberate cruelty, nor was it some random whim of my mother's: Charles really was mad and really was difficult to live with. But we veered, Mum veered, through my childhood, between the fatuousness of hippiedom and the smallness, the meanness of postwar net-curtain twitchery. There was an awful lot we had not thought through. It was uncomfortable for all, horrible for some.

In John Fowles' bestselling novel *Daniel Martin*, published in 1977, the Britain of this era is described as 'a thing in a museum, a dying animal in a zoo'. Fowles quotes Antonio Gramsci's *Prison Notebooks*: 'The crisis consists precisely of the fact that the old is dying and the new cannot be born; in this interregnum a great variety of morbid symptoms appear.' It's a quotation probably due a retirement now: it appears too often describing much common-or-garden morbidity. But it is bang on the money for the 1970s. Charles was paranoid but so was that decade. Tom Wolfe called the 1970s in America 'the Me decade', but in truth, in Britain we hadn't really got to me. Our collective Hillman Minx was stuck on the road between narcissism and old-style duty, between the old-fashioned collective oppression of 'self' and a new flowering of the personal, the internal.

This was still the era of the crowd and proud membership of the crowd, allegiance to it. The mass picket, mass union membership, the block vote, the football throng, the big band, the mass audience TV programme. You could get into crowds that would sweep you off your feet.

There were eddies and flows and you could go with them or kick against them but, whatever your reaction to them was, they were there. Yet there was something else being born, uncomfortably, into this mass age. It was the polar opposite. It was you. Just you. How do *you* feel? What is best for *your* emotional state? There was a shift taking place: social justice – who is up and who is down – was clashing with a new justice of individual self-awareness and self-expression. Don't join the union, take a pill.

Mum flirted with the first but settled, in the end, for the second. Not Ecstasy but Quiet Life (which has been rebranded in the modern age as 'Calm Life', as if they realized the silence of Wells Road was not quite the goal to be promoting) and perhaps the odd Valium. This is why most conventional histories of the 1970s never quite work for me. All the stuff about pickets and strife doesn't capture the self-exploration that was also part of the age, part of Mum's experience of the decade.

Its survivors remember in particular the miners, and the thing they brought us through the 1960s: the coal. The dust that sent miners to early graves settled, albeit less harmfully, on everything. It was everywhere. We smelled it. We smelled of it. We kept it in dank holes under front paths, in hods next to fires. Coal and coke, the processed pebbles, dull and desiccated, that burned hotter. Almost everyone used it. We all knew the sound of it being scooped up, chucked on to fires or into stores. That scraping, scrunching noise as a shovel cut into a pile of it. The satisfying weight of it. If we were to be warm we had to burn it. What was the alternative? Wood? Too expensive and somehow fey: all crackling and pretty flames, not much heat. The other fuels we put in fancy burners these days had not been invented. Electricity? Well, yes, but to produce that, the power stations, too, relied on coal. There was no alternative. It was a coal economy and, more importantly, for a child, it was a coal society. Coal brought us together.

Until it started doing the opposite. At Wells Road our open fire was dispatched with the coming of central heating. A further rift opened up in the relationship between us and working-class people who, among other tasks, risked their health and often gave their lives hacking at the seams and bringing the black chippings to the surface. And just as we were breaking that link, the miners themselves were deciding collectively that the dirty, dangerous job they did might be better paid.

They asked for 25 per cent more. In retrospect, given inflation and previous quiescence, it may well have been a reasonable request. But it felt like a lot and it led to the miners' strike of 1972, the first since the war, and that in turn led to a moment of great import in our lives.

I was too young to know much about the politics of the miners' strike but I knew it resulted in us wrapping Granny in newspaper.

She was cold. She had an electric fire in her room and, as the strike wore on and the power cuts began, Mum and

I were worried. Then one evening on *Blue Peter*, the chairs turned round for this allowable TV programme, Peter Purves and John Noakes showed the watching children how to keep elderly people warm using old papers. They had tabloids but I instantly realized that we, effortlessly superior once again, had broadsheets. In fact, we had two broadsheets for each day: finally our double order of the *Guardian* might be put to good use. I called Mum and we watched together. The next day we bundled up copies of the *Guardian* and put them in our shopping trolley.

I think we took a week's worth of papers to Granny's flat. Mum and I removed the bottom sheet from her mattress, lined it with the paper and replaced the sheet. It crunched a bit but I don't remember her complaining. I enjoyed the idea that we, like cavemen, or soldiers trapped behind enemy lines, were eking out an existence by means of our wits and our resources.*

The newspaper day, however, was a transient pleasure. In the pit of my stomach I knew that everything was falling apart. The miners' strike ended in victory for them and defeat for florid, puffy Edward Heath, the recently elected

---

* I doubt Mum enjoyed it as much. She was not really cut out for survivalism. When the journalist Andy Beckett's brilliant history of the 1970s, *When the Lights Went Out,* was published in 2010, I was delighted to read about the *Blue Peter* episode with the newspaper: proof that I had not imagined or misremembered it. But oh dear ... it seems from Beckett's account that the idea was to place the sheets of paper on top of the elderly person, between two blankets, not underneath, as we had supposed. Mum and I had cocked it up. Hey-ho. Granny survived.

Conservative prime minister. Mum celebrated grimly. It was perplexing, though. The miners were working class, so did not seem to be our people. Yet she loathed Heath more. The reason, looking back, would have been his membership of the class she hated most: the striving lower middle classes. In a way that would have horrified both, she lumped Heath and Thatcher together. The fake mangled posh accent. And, in Heath's case, the acquired taste for classical music (in Mum's Calvinist caste system, betterment was impossible, of course, and the effort contemptible). She would rather back the men with honest dirt under their fingernails than this spiv.

But the collective action side of it? She was a woman apart. She was becoming an individualist. That is what we believed: we were better and there were not many of us. Again, the ambivalence, the Janus vibe, of the whole era: beginnings, ends, transitions, confusions. Facing backwards, facing forwards, outwards, inwards.

We were all stuck, and not in a comfortable place. Francis Wheen's rumbustious transatlantic history of the period, *Strange Days Indeed: The Golden Age of Paranoia*, finishes with an apt description of what he calls 'the peculiar hybrid mood' of the time: 'If the Sixties were a wild weekend and the Eighties a hectic day at the office,' Wheen writes, 'the Seventies were a long Sunday evening in winter, with cold leftovers for supper and a power cut expected at any moment.' An evening, he adds, 'when the wildest thoughts often intrude'.

As a nation we had the wildest of thoughts intruding on mental health; no doubt about that. We knew that something was amiss. We were uncomfortable with the asylums. We were feeling increasingly icky about cruelty, particularly cruelty to children. But we could get no further. The mad were still locked up, kept away, talked about *sotto voce*, if at all. Charles was 'in the community' but not in it as himself. His eyes stared because of the pills he took but you could never tell anyone that, so his eyes just stared. And children were frightened. And, just as the voices in his head told him all sorts of nonsense, there were voices in all of our heads telling us the nonsense was not nonsense at all. Maybe we were mad and he was sane? When my mother heard these things, I wonder what she thought of them? We moved from the humanity of 'close the asylums' to the utter insanity of denying insanity, and did so while treating the whole subject like a bad smell. Nowhere was that 'long Sunday evening in winter' deeper and darker than in our thoughts about madness, and our experience of it at 90 Wells Road.

What would Charles have made of the retired Labour spin doctor Alastair Campbell's modern-day openness about his mental struggles? Of his description of what depression actually feels like?

> Mine has a taste. You know when you have a mild cough or a sore throat and you get yourself some Lockets just to suck on, ease the discomfort and get saliva flowing a

bit? Well, imagine that your mouth feels dry and a bit sore, but instead of Lockets you're sucking on a piece of lead. I don't know what lead tastes like. I am not that mad. But it is how I imagine lead to taste.

One thing strikes me about that passage with the force of a juggernaut. Campbell is open with himself. I am less interested in the feeling, more in his ability to know it. I don't think Charles was allowed to know it. Of course, he could describe the way he felt to a psychiatrist. But outside the room where that private transaction took place there was nowhere for Charles to simply describe his mood, his symptoms. The shame of it was too much. He had to pretend to be 'normal'. To everyone; at work, at home. And in his own head, too. Hence the Bach. But the depth of the shame, the internalized sense of unworthiness, of failure, of anguish and dread? It was so secret that I doubt he could articulate it. Mum told me once that Charles heard voices. He had confided this, but no more. Back then, if you heard voices, you kept quiet. You didn't tell anyone what they said. Not for fear of the voices but of the reaction of the people you told.

It was the garage doors that first gave us away to the neighbours. Doors matter in suburbia. Frosted glass on the front door. Neat gate with a slight squeak. Garage up-and-under. Our garage doors had to be solid because they were guarding the entrance to Hades. They were constructed of wood and required painting. They got chipped.

In a country barn they would have settled happily. But here, in Wells Road, they looked grotesquely out of place. They embarrassed the garage. They swung (when you could get them to move) to a different tune. One set of workmen created huge tension by teasing Charles: 'What you got here then, mate, the Crown Jewels?' But they drilled and sweated to produce the doors demanded and ensure that our garage marked us out. I wondered whether the uniform up-and-under doors might be a working-class preference, but in this instance it seemed unlikely. This was not, for once, a class issue.

A big door requires a big padlock. When Charles died, the collection of giant padlocks we removed from the garage – some as big as a man's hand and an inch thick – would have brought a smile to the face of Houdini. I kept them for years in the vague belief that they might come in useful. But, of course, they did not. The need for that degree of security, outside, perhaps, a lock-up in Dagenham in which lead piping is stored, is limited. It certainly wasn't necessary for our garage, in which a small Hillman Minx, with no radio, was kept.

We forget now how difficult shopping used to be. You had to actually go to the shops. Just as my children don't really understand live TV, they don't understand shopping, except as a kind of sport conducted for fun, for a change. If they really want something, they will buy it, if they can afford it, online. It will be delivered. You don't have to go somewhere and haul it home.

In the 1970s not only was shopping a chore but the shops themselves were still dismal, gloomy little hovels where the best you could hope for if you wanted an item 'not in stock' was that it might be procured within a few weeks. Otherwise, there were supermarkets selling packaged food and places called 'department stores', where lift attendants would call out, 'First floor: women's underwear!' and the nation would giggle. Well, they did at *Are You Being Served?*, the department store sitcom featuring Mollie Sugden as Mrs Slocombe, the senior ladieswear assistant, who spoke often of her cat, Tiddles, which she always referred to as 'my pussy'.

Mrs Slocombe's pussy was (aside from *Morecambe and Wise*) the very apogee of 1970s comedy. Nobody in the country had not seen it. Except us. Its reputation was too smutty. It was not *sensible*.

But, God knows, it was accurate in its depiction of a world of self-serving smallness. A world in which the social structure was all: the customer came last, although he or she could always sit down. Department stores had chairs but little stock.

Ours in Bath was, until it was taken over in 1973, called Colmers (motto: Sterling Value, Small Profits, No Credit). It contained nothing much in the way of saucy jollity that I remember, and, being drapery-based, absolutely nothing that ever interested me, or indeed Charles.

No, if you wanted an item slightly out of the range of the large shop – and that was most things – you had to go to the specialists. Fancy butchers are back in the centres of many of our wealthier towns now, but then they were commonplace and nothing special. You didn't pay extra for bijou surroundings. Bakers, butchers, haberdashers. The high street was still small even if small wasn't, in all cases, beautiful.

For a padlock you went to a hardware shop, an ironmonger. And, for the kind of padlocks Charles was looking for, even in these specialist establishments, a catalogue had to be consulted and orders made. The word 'padlock' conjures up those dainty little articles we use to protect our bikes or to lock sheds. Not for Charles. His were quality pieces of engineering: Sheffield steel, closed-shackle, insurance-rated, weatherproof, marine-grade, fire brigade-grade, unpickable, unliftable without effort, with jailers' keys and utterly impossible to breach once, satisfyingly, the key had been turned with oily finality.

Except that, in his mind, the padlocks were being picked. And, once he decided a lock had been picked, it was no use to him. He would place it in the old chest of drawers he kept at the end of the garage, in front of the Hillman, and buy another. This chest of drawers was a museum of padlocks, all kept with the keys, in case . . . Well, I don't know what he was thinking. But every time he bought a new one he must have wondered at the horror being inflicted: the cost, the humiliation. Over the years the padlocks mounted up and the humiliation with them. I think for a while we were investing in one a month. Only when the Hillman went, some time in the mid-seventies, did the padlocks stop coming.

I hated Charles for the padlocks because of the weirdness they introduced to life. But that was a mistake; one of many. He needed help. To use a blindingly obvious metaphor, but one whose truth simply cries out: he needed a key to a mental padlock. Instead, as the real ones piled up, the mental padlock remained as closed, as tightly bound, as one of those safes you see in bank vaults. There was no way of breaking it: the trick would have been to unpick the lock. Or find a key. But nobody tried.

Charles made one very serious attempt to kill himself. It was on the morning of my twelfth birthday, which we celebrated with bowls of Kellogg's Frosties, a cereal my mother had banned – because of the sugar content – on all other days of the year. But on 3 January we ate Frosties, come what may. They were (and I suppose, are) explosively sugary; little icicles of sweetness baked hard on to cornflakes. They hit home, did Frosties, in the gloom of the era. But on that day they stained the milk light brown as they turned limp in the bowl. Mum had gone upstairs to find out why Charles had not come down and discovered he was unconscious. 'Charles is ill,' she told me. She seemed very calm.

I waited in the sitting room. Might he die? For the second time in my life, I hoped so. For some reason the person who arrived first was Dr Neil, the original bringer of bad news. He briefed the hospital on what might be coming their way:

'not too much effort at resuscitation', was his advice. I am not sure whether I heard him say this or whether Mum told me later but those were the words that she chose to remember about the whole morning. I wanted Charles dead. So, it seems, for all the right reasons, did Dr Neil.

He lived. He had taken a good deal of Valium but not enough to kill him. He was out of hospital in a week and out of his pyjamas after a month. No one ever spoke about it again. I never asked why he had felt this way about his life, and indeed about ours. No effort was made to explain or illuminate. Charles had tried to kill himself, failed, and the Frosties had had to be thrown away.

Actually, he did once allude to it, in a roundabout kind of way, a few months afterwards, in the car on the ten-minute journey to school. 'Everything is beastly,' he said suddenly as we turned too fast round a sharp corner. 'I may not be here for much longer. People are beastly. Do you like birds?'

I replied that I liked puffins, which was the only bird that came to mind and, relieved that this seemed to be the end of the conversation, got out of the car. Some time later, out of the blue, Charles announced that he and I were going to a film showing at a local primary school. It was an RSPB documentary about puffins. I was bored out of my mind as they wandered about some Icelandic hillock with fish, still alive, stuffed in their beaks. There were thousands of them and they looked identical. It was a mysterious evening.

Could I have been a normal stepson? Perhaps. The puffin outing was clearly a rare attempt to connect. But the die had been cast so soon after we met, Charles and I. Mum chose abnormality. I don't think she was ever willing to give anything else a proper chance. I used to come home sometimes, a few minutes after leaving for the walk to school, pretending that I had fallen and hurt my arm. She would let me in and send me back to bed. We would have Heinz tomato soup for lunch. They were the happiest days, just the two of us alone in the house. On one occasion Charles had not yet left for work when I returned with my bizarre excuse for why I should take the day off. He opened the door. 'I suppose you'd better go and be cosseted by your mother,' he said.

Cosseted. The word fascinated me. I asked her what it meant and she was angry, then, with Charles, for belittling our little tacit arrangement. But 'cosseted' was not a bad word. He made no effort to stop it. Mum cosseted me while his job was to put bread on the table and deal with the people who broke into the garage.

In the early seventies, before the Quakerism and the hippiedom and the hankering after Chairman Mao, Mum had experimented with an organization as unflashy as it was decent. She had become a Samaritan. I hated it. It frightened me when she went to a back-street office once a week to talk to people who came in or rang. She told me about the training, the listening you had to do. The potential dangers from people who were beyond help and desperate. It didn't pass me by that we already had such a person at home. Later, I wondered why she didn't spend more time listening to the walk-in case at Wells Road and save herself the bother of a trip into Bath. At the time I didn't want her to do any of it: I wanted to be shot of human mental trauma.

Looking back now, I know – with what little wisdom and distance older age brings – that we let Charles down. I say 'we', because although I went away to boarding school and had little to do with him from then until he died, there must be an age where we accept responsibility for things we have done and not done.

We are all capable of the inconsistencies displayed by those people on Twitter whose self-descriptions are rather belied by the venom of their tweets. 'Vegan, no cruelty,' they say, 'wants only human kindness.' Then you read the tweet: 'Why is this f***** talking such sh**. Ought to be in prison/in hospital/dead.' Often this nice person, who wants only the best for everyone, appears, from their previous online history, to have a tendency to endorse anti-semitism or political assassination. It's common. And, of course, long before social media, it was already common. It's humanity: we are a bit screwed up. Mum would absolutely not have been a social-media warrior – she was genuinely kind. But her concern (sincere and heartfelt) for the victims of dictatorial governments or suicidal tendencies often did not extend to compassion for the person beside her.

And nor did mine. At my dotty, messed-up school I was increasingly serious-minded myself: Amnesty International was a big deal for me, the overthrow of capitalism (I am not so keen these days), the Anti-Nazi League of the later 1970s. But Charles? Who had never really done me any wrong. Who had paid at least some of the bills and lived in obvious and severe mental discomfort. Could I have had a pleasant conversation with him? Just once? I could have, and should have.

But, of course, it is often easier to deal with emotional traumas when they are not part of your life. You can be dispassionate and helpful. At home, amid the smells of madness, with padlocks arriving, food disappearing, Bach blaring, who can blame Mum for the choices she made about this man? But who, in the modern era, would blame him, either?

4

The Age of the Train Set

A deprived child was coming to see us. He lived in London and had never seen cows. This information, passed to me by Mum over breakfast one day, was meant to be the start of a new life. We were going to be sociable. Or at least, I was. There must have been some kind of warning light that had flashed in her mind: 'Justin mustn't be odd.' She thought she had found a way of preventing it and of satisfying her growing interest in the politics of social justice at the same time. She had begun to vote Labour and, although she could not actually join the party, on account of it being a working-class movement, she was becoming keener and keener on Labour and its causes, in inverse proportion to the national mood. But it is fair to say that her social concerns, while genuine, were powered by something closer to home. This deprived boy, this character from *The Road to*

Wigan Pier, was being offered a trip to Bath in the hope that charity would prove a two-way street.

Mum had used the term 'deprived' with no hint of irony. I wondered at it. I was nine or ten and beginning to feel a tad deprived myself; not of food or shelter or physical safety, it is true, and certainly not of a mother's love, but of normality. In Wells Road I had made friends with local children and went to their homes; noisy, chaotic places suffused with the smell of cooking, the sound of bickering siblings, the TV, the chatter of everyday life. The four walls of our home were closing in. The silence was draining my childhood of something vital. Some essence that caused other children to laugh in the street or chew gum or bang each other playfully on the shoulders.

I was terrified, for instance, of birthday parties. It's not that I had no friends; actually, I think I was moderately sociable one to one. But larger social situations, noise, bustle, joshing, being herded around and penned in: all of these things could create an almost physical pain.

I was beginning, just as the deprived child must have been packing, to resent him a little. I had plans to read my encyclopaedia and listen to *Just a Minute* on the radio. So what if he hadn't seen cows? It occurred to me that I hadn't seen cows, either, at least not close up, and it had done me no harm. I was by now the captive of my oddness; trapped in a way that allowed it to be simultaneously a trauma and a comfort. I was becoming aware that things were not right and that although other people had troubles too, they seemed less fundamental, less foundationally shaky. And what could be easier, more soothing, than blocking them out, these jolly outsiders, deprived or not, and sticking with what I knew?

Half an hour before the London boy was due to arrive, I took up a position at the entrance to the shared driveway that led down to our little collection of houses. I waited and waited. Mum was making sausages for lunch. I scanned the passing cars for what I imagined the wan face of deprivation to look like. After an hour Mum came up the drive. The agency had called: the deprived child had cried off. Or had had a better offer. We ate the sausages together in silence and got on with our day. No other invitations were ever made, as far as I am aware, and the whole thing (to use a phrase Mum often used) was 'put down to experience'.

Indeed it was. Soon the day, the wait, the ill-mannered way we had been treated (said Mum) would be forgotten. But the deprived child incident mattered. A lot. It was my personal version of the assassination of the Archduke Franz Ferdinand before the First World War, the act that led to all the dominoes falling across Europe and conflict becoming inevitable, unstoppable. Everything flowed from a single day in 1914 as, for me, everything flowed from that day in (perhaps) 1970. Although we ate our sausages and benefited from having the absentee's portion to share as well, a set of decisions (possibly including the one that sent me to boarding school) seems to me to have taken shape and gathered pace inexorably from this non-event. This chain reaction had all manner of impacts further down the road, impacts stemming from one simple, stark fact: I was alone.

I have one minor but genuinely unusual talent that holds its own even among people who read for a living: I can read off a page with no hint that reading is taking place. Words flow in and flow out. It's a fluency that began in those long days when the only thing moving in our home was the dust, caught in sunlight, gradually falling towards the floor as Mum and I read aloud together, chapter after chapter. Jennings dropped at silly mid-on, scoring his century and basking in the congratulations of the cricket team. Paddington getting his head stuck in a jar, or painting his room white and being unable to find the door, but nobody minding and everyone being pleased in the end, and having a lovely supper cooked by Mrs Bird. I think I read aloud more in those early years than most radio announcers do in a lifetime. Mum used to fall asleep but I would plough on and on, the silence of the house broken only by my small voice.

Alone, with one eye on escape and one eye on Mum, I was destined to wander the world always half looking for adventure, half wondering what on earth I was doing so far from home, so solitary, so strange.

My first major trip without my mother was at the age of fourteen or fifteen. She had bought me a bike for Christmas. It was, like so many of her gifts, a good deal less glitzy than advertised. I had friends at school who claimed they had five-gear bikes in the shed at home, with drop handlebars and a racy look. Mum did not approve of a racy look. I got an upright, hugely heavy, three-geared affair. A kind of Hillman Minx on two wheels. Still, even with only three gears, it afforded hitherto unguessed-at opportunities. Principally, opportunities to be alone. To get away. I could cycle, in first gear and with satisfying, muscle-tweaking effort, out of the bowl in which the city of Bath sits, out into the countryside. Then zoom back down wide Georgian streets. It was a new freedom, a new form of isolation coupled with movement.

Bored during a long summer holiday, and by now properly energized by cycling, I decided to try to ride from Bath to East Coker at the other end of Somerset. This is a four- or five-hour journey by bike, involving main roads, steep hills, country lanes. I had never cycled for more than an hour before. I had never left Bath and its environs alone, except to go to school. It was a real adventure. A journey undertaken entirely for its own sake.

Why East Coker? It is not on the youth trail, East Coker. Never was, never will be. There is nothing there. Well, not quite nothing. We had called in years before at St Michael's Church, stained-glass windows, whitewashed walls, barren pews, empty and damp-smelling, where T. S. Eliot is buried. It had been a sudden decision of Charles's to veer off the route home from a day trip to Bournemouth, where my aunt was then living. We gazed at those two famous lines curving round the top and bottom of the oval memorial plaque: 'in my beginning is my end' and 'in my end is my beginning'.

I was way too young for Eliot. Mum was annoyed that we'd stopped there; thought it a silly conceit that had brought her mad husband on this pilgrimage. But I was transfixed. My beginning. My end. And the flow of the lines, the momentousness of it all. In the churchyard there is a gravestone commemorating seventy parishioners who died of the plague between June and September 1645. For Mum, I pretended to be bored. But East Coker was filed away in the mind of a young boy, perhaps eight or nine, for further inspection.

However, the church was not my mission this time. There was also a cottage I knew in East Coker, a middle cottage in a thatched terrace of four or five, with miniature front gardens separated from the lane by little child-sized gates. The only surviving picture of me as a young boy was taken there. I am wearing shorts, a woollen jumper over a smart shirt, and an expression that says, 'Hello, why are we taking photos? We never take photos.'

The photograph does not do justice to that little cottage or to my feelings about being there. It is the place where I spent some of the happiest hours of my young life. I wanted to stay for ever in East Coker.

It was a tiny house. Adults had to stoop to enter. On the right there was a chintzy little sitting room with an open fire. On the left, a parlour, over-filled with cabinets containing china and a formal dining table. Only one person at a time could go in and back out again. Straight ahead was a kitchen, a galley affair added on to the cottage a century or so before, with a door leading to a long, over-grown garden.

And Mrs Lock was at the door.

Mrs Lock had never heard of T. S. Eliot. That was invariably the joke in the Hillman on the way down to East Coker. Imagine . . . Not a word of him. Not a book in the cottage. But she was a dear old thing and it was right to go and see her.

Who was she? I have absolutely no idea. I think she might have been the mother of a friend of Mum's from bygone years. The friend was not around – dead, perhaps? In my memory there was never a Mr Lock, but if there was a daughter, surely there had been a husband. And why did Mrs Lock live here, a place where a bus came only on market days and even then went only to Yeovil? Why did no one else visit? But perhaps they did: children see uniqueness where there's ubiquity because the ubiquity is beyond their gaze. Perhaps people came every day, other families from other moments in this old lady's past.

But I doubt it. There was something about these Saturday afternoons that suggested duty on the part of my mother, resignation on the part of Charles and a joyousness in Mrs Lock that spoke of a hugely welcome break from winter evenings alone with her photographs. For someone with no past (that I was aware of), she had a lot of photographs. I noticed them because, back in Bath, we had none. I suppose Mum had albums, but there was nothing on display. Mrs Lock had dozens of pictures, perhaps a hundred, each lovingly encased in a small frame. They covered every space of the cottage, every shelf, little occasional tables, the sill of the thick front wall into which the window had been cut. The mantelpiece above the fire. All faded, many black and white. Weddings, holidays, visits before, I assumed, the visits stopped; unsmiling figures, many of them wearing the kind of sombre expression early twentieth-century people adopted to pose for the camera, as if they thought it uncouth to waste the moment of their immortalization with something as gauche as a grin.

Mrs Lock was skeletal, hunched, covered in layers of cardigans that hung over a tweedy skirt and dark thick tights. She had a reedy, raspy voice and a Somerset accent – 'Ooh, my dear,' she would croak when we arrived, 'grown again! So big, so strong!' – and she would hug me as only she, Mum and Granny could hug.

There was a ritual to our visits. First, after the greetings and the invitation to use the tiny lavender-scented loo at the top of the stairs, we would settle in the sitting room, Mrs Lock on her chair by the window, Mum and Charles on the mini-sofa (this was the closest they ever had to sit; it was the closest I ever saw them), and me on the carpet in front of the fire. There would be a general discussion of people of whom I had never heard. Then, gloriously, came the lighting of the fire. I was allowed to use a match. She had prepared it, the kindling, the larger logs. They spat and crackled and I stared. Afire. Unpredictable, noisy, rumbustious, and inside the house. The sterility of our existence at home shown up for what it was: less than fully living. I was allowed to feed the fire with logs. I imagined myself as the fireman on the footplate on *The Flying Scotsman*, hurtling north, keeping the fire stoked, face hot and dirty.

This lasted for an hour or more. And then came the next stage of this highly choreographed day in the country. Mrs Lock would suggest it was time for tea.

We did not eat cakes. I was allowed them on special occasions and at home a 'chocolate and sweets' jar was brought out after meals from which I could take an acceptable, moderate ration. But the idea of biscuits or cakes eaten carelessly alongside a cup of tea or coffee was too ordinary for us. Ordinary in the sense of both normal and common. We were neither.

But with Mrs Lock we were allowed to be. I really had never seen anything like it. Sweet bread with raisins, cut into thin slices and served under swirls of yellow butter. A cake with glacé cherries in it, so firm that when it was cut, the cherries sliced too, in perfect cross-section. Fruit cake. Biscuits. Scones with cream and jam. All laid out on the table in the parlour, where we went, one by one, to make our choice and bring back our selection to eat in front of the fire. Food and pleasure. Everyone on best behaviour because, in a doll-sized cottage, with your head constantly in danger from the beams and a crackling open fire, with Mrs Lock fussing, even we were normal.

She would see us off from the gate, waving till we disappeared, she disappeared, from view.

East Coker, then, was my trip of choice. It had been a year or so since we had been to see Mrs Lock. The visits had come to an end when Charles stopped driving. Perhaps Mum felt guilty and encouraged me to go there. Perhaps I really did have no one else to visit. Or perhaps I did, but still preferred the comforting certainty represented by a little old lady in a rural cottage, the tea, the meaningless chat, the uncomplicated affection.

I set off with Mum's emergency sustenance, a slice of nut roast packed elaborately in tinfoil and placed in a pannier, a bottle of water from the tap, an Ordnance Survey map of Somerset and a puncture repair kit in a little tin. The nut roast is worth dwelling on: Mum could only cook two dishes. The first was 'sausages in cider', from some cookbook endorsed by Fanny Cradock; the second, much finer and accorded the longevity due to its tastiness and health-giving qualities, was the nut roast. It was not subtle: caramelized onions provided its one dominant flavour, hazelnuts (cheap) its bulk. We ate it, off and on, until she died. But if I tasted it again, the day I left for East Coker would be the day to which it transported me back.

The open road. Did I call home when I arrived? I slightly doubt it; or perhaps I reversed the charges, as I did from school. Mrs Lock was as solicitous as ever and as genuinely delighted to have a visitor. I felt like a cross between Ernest Shackleton and one of those intrepid chaps in the First

World War who traversed no-man's-land to get an urgent message to a trapped squadron. I had ridden a bike across the badlands of Somerset, through Radstock and close to Yeovil. I could survive on my own. And if it were possible on this relatively modest expedition, might it be possible, psychologically and practically, in tougher circumstances, too?

A normal boy would have been ill-equipped to cope with the evening that ensued. But I was made for this kind of situation: an old lady, an odd meal, consisting mainly of cabbage, cooked in the 1950s tradition – heavy boiling followed by the application of butter in a futile attempt to make it more palatable. An entire evening of small talk about people of whom I knew nothing, had never met and never would. Leyla and Leslie. Dorothy, with her heart. Richard and Susie: his legs, her small business. On and on and on it went. I was fine with it. I could laugh in the face of tortured vegetables. Nothing at home (and nothing at school) involved the application of culinary imagination. Mum had all the inattention to taste (of the tongue-captured variety) for which the English upper classes have always been noted. And as for the conversation: if feigning interest were an Olympic sport I would, in my mid-teens, already have been a multiple gold medallist.

And so to bed. I had brought a toothbrush. We said goodnight and I withdrew to the spare room at the top of the cottage, a room where every surface was covered by needlework, 'fancywork' as it would have been known in

Mrs Lock's heyday. Bedside tables with thick embroidery. A bedspread, several footstools, lampshades, all intricately sewn or crocheted, presumably by Mrs Lock's own hand. Samplers on the wall. All so delicate, so feminine, yet at the same time so utterly sexless, dry, desiccated, artless. I had forgotten pyjamas and she seemed to have forgotten sheets, or had expected me to bring a sleeping bag. Reluctant to be naked against the sinews of Mrs Lock's sewing, I slept with my clothes on.

In the morning we breakfasted on Rice Krispies. I was ready to make for home before the questions about why I had made this trip penetrated my mind. We said a genuinely affectionate goodbye. I think we both knew we would never see each other again. And we never did.

On the way back something strange happened. I stopped in a place called Paulton to eat the rest of the nut roast, which I had saved for the return journey. Paulton is a grey, tired village with a main street too narrow for the weight of traffic that goes through it and a disease-like spread of rain-spattered housing round about. This was the era of mining in Somerset, and Paulton was as depressed and gloomy as any mining town anywhere in Britain. I bought a drink to accompany my meal, sat in a bus shelter, began to eat the nut roast and suddenly had a physical urge to be sick. Amid the gloom, the mid-seventies tawdriness, I felt trapped. Gasping for air. I toyed with the idea of not going home. Not seriously, of course, but the possibility occurred to me in the way it does to adolescents with the shock of their first realization that they have agency to a hitherto unknown extent. You can come off the road. You can stop when and where you like. You could take a completely different road.

Or you can just pedal off. That's what I did – I pedalled off, straight into a passing car.

I think it had been trying to overtake me but, on noticing an oncoming Ford Escort, and to avoid a head-on collision, the driver swerved in towards me just at the moment I was pulling out into the main carriageway. It was a low-speed accident and I had the view of it that I would have of other, future crashes – a not unpleasant, almost euphoric, hallucinogenic sense that something was happening to my body which I was watching from a safe distance.

Somehow I stayed upright, but I careered over the pavement and into a dip that led down into a field, where I parted company with my bike.

Did the car driver just assume I was OK? Or did he or she think that I was not OK and that was the reason why they didn't stop? Had no one else seen the collision? The bike was undamaged apart from a few scrapes. I felt bruised but I could walk. I was embarrassed, mainly, and then something else – thrilled perhaps is the right word – when it dawned on me that there were no witnesses at all to this incident. Paulton is, at the best of times, sleepy. It's the epitome of keep-yourself-to-yourself England. Perhaps someone had seen but had turned away. I had diced with death alone. No one knew but me. I was, in retrospect, in shock. Having heaved the bike back to the roadside, I went back into the brambles in the field to try to retrieve the nut roast. I couldn't find it. I cried.

After a half-hour or so, I set off on my journey home.

There is a connection, isn't there, between the ability of a human being to move freely and a sense of well-being. 'Music and Movement' was, I remember, the name of an activity at infants' school. My Uncle Oliver used to laugh about it: boxing would be better for boys, he believed. Not just because it was more manly. It also helped you to learn to stand your ground. Deal with the enemy. Defend territory. Avoid advancing beyond the reach of the supply lines. The old hypocrite: he had driving gloves and maps of all of England. Although I doubt he ever thought about it, about anything much, he would have viscerally understood the great truth about our desire to escape, to break free from life. We are not 'born free but everywhere in chains', as Rousseau would have us believe. We are born in chains, of family and circumstances and genes, but sometimes, gradually, achieve a measure of freedom over the course of a life. For centuries, for all of human history until relatively recently, no one actually went very fast and few went very far. But my generation, not postwar but post-postwar, was a generation born to travel and to travel fast.

Concorde was in the air. It was, Jimmy Savile told us, the 'Age of the Train'. Trailfinders was set up in a shop in Earls Court. The M25 was planned and looked forward to; bits of it were even completed, though we didn't get the whole orbit of London until 1986. But we absorbed the message, from Mrs Thatcher, rising to prominence with every passing year of the decade, Mrs Thatcher, who would one day open the full motorway, that private cars brought with them private freedom. An Escort in the garage. Even a Hillman Minx. But the mode of transport was not the main issue: from the hippie trail to Afghanistan to the commute to Charing Cross, people were increasingly on the move. We forget what a change this was from the life so recently lived by so many. In spite of the fact that there was a train every hour every day, from a station ten minutes' walk away, making a trip lasting less than an hour and forty-five minutes, with a buffet car supplied and a rudimentary lavatory, too, our next-door neighbours in Bath had never been to London.

Nor had I. My early years were the age of the train set.

The piecing together of which had begun painfully slowly. Mum understood nothing practical, certainly nothing about trains, and had not realized that track, when laid, would have to join up with itself. Otherwise the train could only shuttle a short distance and would keep stopping. Which would be no fun. It meant that the Christmas present of the first pieces of track and a green steam engine were not the unparalleled success they might have been. Mum? We went back to the shop as soon as it opened in January and sorted ourselves out. First: never mind steam. This was not some kind of olde-worlde legacy celebration.

I wanted diesel, preferably faithful facsimiles of the diesels that heaved and juddered not far from the bottom of our garden. I wanted something rooted in real. So we bought a Class 31, one of the least glamorous engines ever to have graced a British track. It looks like a box, with a stubby flat front. And for carriages I got replicas of the exact carriages trundling past our window: British Rail blue-and-white Intercity stock.

We acquired enough track for two concentric ovals to be assembled and a board for them to go on. This was vital: it was to be a track that described real life as I could visualize it; the escape in my head. Not for me something fancy with bridges and plastic cows in fields. It was a flat piece of white board with a station and some signals, not faux-realistic but representational, emblematic. I had no time for mise-en-scène – there was work to be done.

The word obsession is overused but I was, once the track was in place and the proper locomotive bought, obsessed with the creation of a world around it that existed in my imagination and involved an intricate pattern of arrivals and departures – particularly departures. I constructed, with painstaking care, the timetables of a fake domain. I knew the geography of Dorset and south Somerset and I pictured my railway as connecting this part of the world to Yeovil and London. I was the Anti-Beeching. Although I had never heard of the man whose plans destroyed the country railway in so many corners of Britain, I was creating a little of the realm he consigned to history.

My trains were frequent and well run. They began work at around five in the morning, with last journeys for part of the route late at night. If you wanted to get from Cerne Abbas to Dorchester after 11pm you were out of luck. And in the morning there was a Pullman service that stopped nowhere, with a slower train beginning its trip just a few minutes after the fast one taking the same route. Folks: this is how railways work! I was a visionary. A timetabler. All of this written in neat columns on pieces of paper stapled together to look like the annual timetable published by British Rail.

This was all the more of an achievement because I could barely write. Not in the sense of being illiterate, of course: Mum would have been on to that. But in the more practical sense of being unable to communicate using pen and paper. Nobody ever knew how I came to be put up a year at my prep school and thus failed to learn this useful skill. I had finished infants' school and was due to move on to the state primary but by now Mum had other ideas. She told me later that she had asked to look round the primary school and it was when the headteacher told her his pupils included the children of doctors that she had decided to bail. Nothing offended her more than chippiness among the lower orders. The actual presence of doctors' children would have pleased her but the need to talk about it she thought uncouth, unbecoming, embarrassing. So, in a fit of pique, she removed me and placed me instead at the Park Preparatory School for Boys, a gloomy outpost of Victorian education in which the children of Bath's richer shopkeepers and farmers were groomed for a life at public school.

Perhaps I arrived between terms. Whatever the case, I began in a class in which no one, including me, could write in longhand. Then one day I was summoned to the front and told to take my satchel with me: I was going up a class. In this class my fellow pupils could already write and, crucially, read longhand script. I could not. I said nothing. I did my best. Mum, who had beautiful handwriting, tried to help. But it was never going to work. One more isolating step had been taken. A friend of mine had a similar experience in Wales. Sent by careless parents to a Welsh-language school in his early years, and speaking not a word of it, he would look out of the window and build an imaginary world. He is now a novelist. We live with the cards we are dealt. Mine were solitude and an inability to write. The work-arounds were typing and . . . Well, what?

My train obsession was never about spotting engines. It was about spotting whole trains, people, destinations, departures. We would go to Bristol sometimes, a fifteen-minute trip from Bath, to sit at the end of the huge Temple Meads station and watch as locomotives brought in arrivals from Newcastle en route for Penzance, from Torbay hoping to make Liverpool by nightfall. Trainspotters would note the numbers of the engines (why? I have never understood it) but this little boy would be transfixed by the trains themselves. Dusk was the best time (Mum looking at her watch and suggesting we called it a day), with long-range departures about to be made for Edinburgh or Plymouth. The faces of the passengers in the glow of the lighted carriages. The mixture of tiredness and excitement that a long journey can bring. They would sleep that night unimaginable miles away from this humdrum place. They were lugging themselves towards things, away from things. Above all, they were moving.

There is something in a static life, an enervated life, that cries out for all of this.

And in a lonely life, too. The train obsession was both a result and a begetter of loneliness. Not that this mattered to me. In fact, it allowed a greater concentration on what really mattered: whether the 06:54 from Dorchester to London was on time on my track. And, concurrently, whether the real-life 17:30 from Bristol to London was passing my window at 17:45 and so was also on time. And if not, why not? I invented the most intricate of worlds, with one foot in the real railway visible from my bedroom window and the other in the train set network of Dorset stations served by my diesel engine and its carriages. Neither of these foundations could be accessible to anyone else. Others could not have understood for a minute why they mattered. I would not have wanted to explain. I could not have explained.

Of course, there is nothing wrong with the ownership of a personal world. We all have one. Maybe even a secret imaginary friend or two. Pixies at the bottom of the garden. The creation at 90 Wells Road was not special in imaginative terms but in the degree of its separation from all else.

At some stage in my early life (I have no idea when and my medical records don't show it) I went into hospital for a few days to have my adenoids removed. This is a routine operation on the throats of children whose adenoids become swollen after bad colds or other infections – I think these days it's done in a day and no one breaks stride. In the late 1960s, when Mum and Dr Neil must have decided it was right for me, it involved incarceration in a children's ward. Matrons were still stern in those days; beds hard and crammed together in a Nissen hut. The whole procedure uncomfortable and vaguely frightening for a young child, any child.

But all I remember of the whole thing is one moment. They took the toys I had brought in with me (two buses and a van) and put them in the middle of the ward to be shared with the other children. It was devastating. For all the copies of the *Guardian* that piled up at home, I had never come across the actual sharing side of socialism in real life. I had never come across society. I didn't cry. I was way too shocked. Mum, when she arrived, retrieved the vehicles and packed them away. I had lost my adenoids but kept my separateness. It might have been better if it had been the other way round.

On my eighteenth birthday, at the beginning of 1979, I conducted an experiment. Presents had rather dried up in recent years. Uncle Oliver had never believed in them and

Aunt Charmion, not unreasonably, felt she had done her bit. Mum gave me a paperback thesaurus. Knowing in advance that it was not going to be a day of merry-making and gasp-worthy surprises, I had decided that I would mark it by taking myself, alone, to a pizza restaurant and eating as many as I could manage. I managed two. I think I wanted to throw up: and, in throwing up, throw away all that had been and start again. Loneliness is not the absence of people or even, often, the absence of friends. It's more a state of mind. It can co-exist with the ability to perform, chat, function, succeed. I wondered that day if I could kick the state of mind. Perhaps it was time to be someone different. To achieve a transition, embark on a transformative change of scene. Perhaps, but not yet. There was nowhere to go that afternoon but home. 'Did you enjoy it?' Mum asked.

5

Are You OK to Carry On?

Early on a chilly Monday in December 1976, an ambulance was summoned to Sidcot School. The school stretches across a couple of acres of rising ground in the gentle, slightly suburban countryside of the Mendip Hills south of Bristol. The A38, the main road, bends around it. In the 1970s Sidcot had the bleak, municipal look of an apparently accidental agglomeration of buildings, none of them showing an interest in the outside world. A private place, a secret society. A passing motorist may have taken it for a laundry or an open prison. If you had an appointment, or a sentence to serve, a lane would take you off the main road, past the Georgian-style Meeting House on the left, the school entrance on the right. The lane itself went nowhere: on up a hill until it petered out and became farmland.

On this morning it had been snowing and the road and lane were silent. We could hear the siren miles away. When it arrived and nosed past the swimming pool into the central courtyard, the vehicle's blue lights flashed manically in icy windows.

There had been an explosion in the chemistry lab, a high-roofed room, smelling faintly of rotten eggs, in an older, red-brick block under a clocktower in the centre of the school. It had a Victorian schoolroom vibe: wooden benches and huge windows that seemed, in spite of their size, incapable of letting in proper light. The panes were cracked, the upper reaches covered in layer upon layer, generation upon generation, of chemical residue. On the wall opposite the windows there were floor-to-ceiling cabinets with glass doors. Dusty test tubes stood in wooden holders. There was a huge white basin at the front of the lab, stained and plug-less. All of this was the personal fiefdom of Aubrey Hope, the chemistry teacher. Mr Hope was a tiny Welsh speck of a man with huge ears and a dangerously violent temper. The only way of getting into his good books was 'working' for him, which meant doing his preparations so that he didn't have to bother.

That year he had offered the job of lab technician to three boys (girls were not heavily involved in chemistry at Sidcot), who had to make sure the chemicals were ready for the junior pupils by the time classes began each day. They were presented with a key to the lab. In truth, this was a waste of time as there were several master keys in the possession of the pupils which allowed us liberal access to the whole school, every room, every exam paper storage site, everywhere.

Anyway, using their official key, on this day the 'lab technicians' had entered the chemistry lab and, moments later, blown themselves up. They had been handling, with no goggles, no supervision and not much care, a store of red phosphorus. More than handling, in fact. Knowing that red phosphorus burns with a rather satisfactory glow, and not having much to do that day before breakfast, they added a selection of other chemicals to the mix with the idea of smuggling the concoction out of school into the nearby fields and setting it alight. Among the chemicals they chose was crystalline iodine which, when added to phosphorus, can spontaneously combust.

It did. My friend Patrick was the closest and was burned on his hands and face. Rather wonderfully, his first words after the explosion were, 'Is there any chance of us getting away with this?'

There was and there wasn't. Nothing encapsulated the oddness, the dysfunction of the 1970s better than the experience of an education provided in that era by the Religious Society of Friends. Sidcot School was one of a group run by the Friends, the sect colloquially known from their birth as the Quakers. As such it was meant to be kindly and stolid, like the Quakers themselves. The 2020 edition of the *Good School Guide* tells us: 'For those untroubled by notions of social pretension or academic snobbery, yet for whom a considerate altruistic atmosphere really matters, this is just the place.'

I am genuinely glad for the school and for the pupils there today. I am glad especially about the altruism.

It wasn't like that when I was there. It was grim. It was lost. A place of despair. A wrecker of already damaged lives.

There were 360 boys and girls and a handful of teachers, several of whom would have recognized themselves in Evelyn Waugh's fictional North Wales prep school hellhole in *Decline and Fall*.

The school smelled of polish and sweat and overcooked greens. There was not a single carpet in the whole of the boys' side of the building. There were no pictures on the walls, which were painted industrial dark red or brown. Lockers were metal, padlocked shut. The centrepiece was a shed – 'the boys' shed'. Down one side of it there were large windows looking across to the clocktower above the chemistry lab. Off it, on the inside, was a classroom for the youngest children. A staircase, internal and unlit, ascended to form rooms for older children. The whole place was a mass of badly painted wood. If I went underground down some stone stairs in one corner and through an unlit tunnel, I could cross to the 'girls' side', where there was a corresponding 'girls' shed', lighter and softer because, in the 1970s, girls were lighter and softer (or meant to be). It had table-tennis tables. A small, dark-wood-panelled library. And, on the walls, those formal scholarship boards that posh schools have.

The school had a games field but it was a short walk away – a walk that gave the briefest of glimpses of the outside world. We had to cross a bridge over the A38 to reach it. Every time I did so, I was struck by how fast the cars beneath my feet seemed to be going, in a world utterly separate from ours. Off to see Mum. Home for tea. Up to Bristol. Even in later years, by which time I was quite institutionalized, I recall looking down at the passing traffic, wondering about the lives it contained.

We slept in huge dormitories, at least forty of us to a room. No privacy, no individuality, no mercy for those who fell by any kind of wayside. We were corralled like animals. We were woken by bells.

A Woody Allen character once declared himself so unheroic he had been 'beaten up by Quakers'. At my school we would not have got the joke.

Draw a veil over the chemistry block explosion and pick another day: it's June, the summer term of 1975. The school was seething. The anguish of the nation, teetering on the brink of collapse, reverberating around our collapsing estate. This day began with an insurrection at the start of morning assembly – something to do with bedtimes or haircuts – which ended only when the aforementioned and ironically named chemistry master, Mr Hope, waved what he claimed, at the top of his voice, was a loaded pistol. Lessons were suspended and fifth-formers smoked cannabis and snogged in their hide-outs overlooking the playground, to the strains of Free's 'All Right Now'. The younger kids, worried and excited in equal measure, were kept in classrooms while the school waited to see what became of the revolution. Nothing was all right, that was for sure. No more all right than it was in the song.

The previous afternoon had seen a concerted attack on a female biology teacher with Bunsen burners, their rubber tubes detached from the gas supply and attached to the taps so that they delivered targeted hoses of water. She had fled in tears and there had been a fight when the serious people at the front of the class who wanted to learn things had taken her side. I hadn't witnessed this because I'd been suspended from biology lessons for suggesting insolently, in a test, that the alimentary canal went from London to Liverpool and had recently been restored and dredged by the London to Liverpool Alimentary Canal Society.

Mr Hope finally restored some order and the insurrection petered out into a tense teatime and eventually the quiet of night. But Sidcot School then was not a place for the faint-hearted or the academically ambitious.

Online trolls sometimes discover that I went to a fee-paying boarding school and post triumphant messages suggesting that I have no ability to question Tory Privilege or American Imperialism because I had such a privileged upbringing myself. I suppose they imagine tuck boxes and wall games and younger boys bringing me freshly buttered toast. A life of bumping into buffers one had joshed with in the common room; of banking with pals who are 'something in the City' and know where the best deals are to be had; of 'anything for you, old man – we were blood brothers in the lower school'.

I wish it had been like that. We didn't even have hot water. At mealtimes, the eldest and strongest took the best food. This was not by chance or against the rules: the older children sat at the end of long *Tom Brown's Schooldays*-style tables and benches with the younger pupils in the middle. The older ones served the food and passed down the plates, small portions, spat-in portions, handed out to eleven-year-olds in thrice-daily lessons in the rawness of power relationships. There was a butter obsession at Sidcot. People grabbed the stuff from dishes and covered everything with it, baked beans, fish, meat. It was comfort perhaps: butter that at home had been spread daintily on bread. Butter with a sweet, dependable taste. A smothering taste, overwhelming, overcoming.

In my later days at the school I became a vegetarian to avoid the poisonous semi-cooked sausages on which most of us lived. When I try now to make my kids eat food marginally beyond its sell-by date they raise their eyes to the sky and mouth, 'Daddy went to boarding school.'

My private-school life never felt privileged. If I had ever thought about it, I would have yearned for actual privilege: for a home with parents and a life in a nice comprehensive like the one my wife went to, where all the children of the lecturers at the local university formed their own cosy group and holidayed together in camper vans before gliding off effortlessly to other, top universities.

Quakerism is extraordinary. It began in seventeenth-century England, among dissenters from the Church of England who decided that God could speak, did speak, to all of us individually. We were all the priesthood and should all live lives of priestly piety. And many Quakers did. They refused to swear oaths (they still do) because they want it assumed that they always tell the truth. Among the other things they don't like are war and gambling. They are very keen on peace and prudence. There's a fine old Quaker phrase, first used by their founder George Fox, 'Walk cheerfully over the world, answering that of God in Everyone.' In my schooldays the word 'cheerful' always struck me as ill-suited to the Quakers I knew. In fact Quakerism was in flux. It was indeed an austere sect – there is no evidence that George Fox was a barrel of laughs – but, during the last century, it was in the process of lightening up, following the same path as liberalism: sturdy, self-reliant and individualistic in its early incarnation before becoming more socially focused, prizing equality more and the individual less.

The Quakers of the 1970s, then, were an earnest, peaceful sect who meant no one any harm and hoped fervently that all should get along with all. They were mostly middle class, mostly white. The women were stout, the men spindly. Strangers to fashion, they wore layers of beige clothes, their hair was grey or salt-and-pepper, their shoes (Clarks is a famous old Quaker company) far from Manolo Blahnik. Often the men had a wild, eccentric look, as if playing the part of an Oxbridge don in a film, but they were twin-kly, too: the Quakers, while falling a little short of cheerful, smiled more than most people did in that decade.

Every week the whole school would troop into Sunday Meeting in the school theatre to be smiled at and improved.

Here we were joined by Quakers from the village and an entire hour would be spent alone with our thoughts. Even when some elderly Friend took to her feet and revealed, slowly, ponderously, that she had been shopping that week and lost the butter before getting it home, leaving us tee-tering in expectation of the punchline 'Life's a lot like that . . .', the sense of anticipation only marginally assuaged the boredom. There was nowhere to hide from its inten-sity. The impact of this on me has been wholly positive. I'm comfortable with silence. I have never listened to a podcast. I seek no soundtrack, no clutter, feel no FOMO. I am self-contained. The silence began at home, to be sure. But it carried on, week after week, into late adolescence. I am happy in situations where a pin dropped is a mighty disorder. I am grateful to the Quakers for honing the skill of not moving a muscle and just thinking thoughts.

That said, it often seemed like the most exquisite tor-ture. Rows of us sat on benches covered with long, thin, blue leather cushions. These were the cheap seats that rose above the stage; the old folk from the village (to us they all seemed old, and I think they probably were) had their own space on chairs set out on the polished floorboards of the well between the benches and the stage. Quakers don't do hymns or sermons but boy, do they do silence. If Green-landers have a thousand words for snow the Quakers could have a million for silence. For the restless, settling silence as 300 children come to terms with the fact that they are going to be alone with their thoughts for an hour. The slightly giggly silence as knowing glances are exchanged. The concentrated silence emanating from adolescent boys trying to look down the fronts of the girls sitting in the slightly lower tiers in front of them. The silence fractured by children getting bored and dropping coins on the floor. Or silence shattered to the extent that punishment is required, for example, by letting a marble fall down the stairs to the gallery level to roll all the way through the slightly flatter levels until it comes to rest in the well under the chair of an ancient local person. Who pretends not to notice. Who may not actually notice, owing to entrance-ment or deafness or both.

When they did notice, they might decide to use this as what the Americans now call a 'teachable moment'. A craggy, leather-skinned chap once rose to his feet like an Old Testament prophet, a visitor from the distant past, and it felt as if a condemnation was about to be issued that might change the shape of our Sunday evening quite con-siderably, with mass detention, perhaps, or the offering up of the guilty, replacing tea and *The Golden Shot* in TV hour.

'Marbles,' he began, 'are a source of fun. And we need to be able to have fun.' And then he sat down. After this, no punishment was possible. Someone giggled. It was as inexplicable as everything seemed to be in those days. But once he had spoken and the silence descended anew (God, I sound like a Quaker but bear with me), it was a different kind of silence again, a deeper silence. We tend in the modern world to think of silence as an absence: the absence of noise. But silence – especially Quaker silence – can be much more than that. It is a thing in itself. As Matthew Crawford puts it in his book *The World Beyond Your Head*: 'The benefits of silence are off the books. They are not measured by any econometric instrument such as gross domestic product, yet the availability of silence surely contributes to creativity and innovation ... One consumes a great deal of silence in the course of becoming educated.' We at Sidcot certainly did. More was learned through the silence than the teaching, I suspect. The Quakers imparted wisdom that the staff, in the main, did not possess.

But here is the paradox of Quakerism in the 1970s. There is no fire and brimstone in the soul of the sect. They had, by the end of the nineteenth century, entirely abandoned the preachiness of their early life and although they were hardly gay (in the old sense), they were socially liberal to a fault. They wanted to release prisoners from prison. They wanted to release the poor from poverty. They wanted to release the world from war. They wanted women to be equal to men. They wanted freedom for the oppressed. They valued kindness and peace.

And yet here they were running a school in which children were tortured.

I use the word advisedly. The torture was both physical and mental. I think of the howls, an animal noise I can still hear today, of a boy I will call David. I can still smell him: a faint whiff of urine and a stronger one of sweat. He seemed always to be sweaty, always on the run. David, who probably had what we would now call learning difficulties, had been held back a year and was in the exquisitely awful position of having once been senior but now being junior. He received the kind of treatment a top policeman might get when sent to jail.

It had been decided by the thugs who ran the boys' side of the school that David was gay. He had been caught (they claimed) having sex with another boy in the changing rooms. He was marked, stained. Destined to live every day under the cosh. Every minute. Anyone who was with him was taken aside and given the chance to repent or face the same fate. That fate was partly physical – he was made to sit in the showers while boys cracked the top of his head with their knuckles until he cried. He was chased and kicked. He was pushed down stairs, chairs were taken from under him as he was about to sit down. All of this and more, but the physical paled to insignificance compared with the mental torture to which he was subjected. He was a pariah at the age of twelve. A leper at thirteen. A dead man walking at fourteen. By fifteen, a beaten dog, a hollowed-out person, a loser who had internalized his status. An untouchable. His face, as we got older, became haunted. He haunts me still because I did absolutely nothing to help him.

His only escape was his roller skates. They had thick rubber wheels and buckles to get them firmly fixed to the outside of school shoes. From the main playground down to the lower level, next to the modern classroom block, there was a ramp for cars and delivery vehicles. It was steep and ended in a sharp bend. David would enter it as fast as he could and head for the corner, just managing to turn at the last moment. Again and again. On his own. Leaving only when the bullies arrived, jeering 'Bummer David!' Some time before the sixth-form term began, he didn't come back, and nobody heard any more of him.

And the teachers? Did they ever intervene? Perhaps, though we were unaware of it. Maybe behind the scenes they kept David alive. If it was true that he was gay, they could retrospectively plead that homosexuality was a source of fear and loathing difficult to imagine in today's Britain. It filled people with disgust. To take any other view would have been eccentric. It had been legal for only a handful of years and few people were 'out' – this was the Britain of the Jeremy Thorpe trial, of public lavatories where men took chances with their reputations, their careers, their lives. And yet it was also the Britain of what we would now call queer culture, of Marc Bolan, of David Bowie, of a subterranean sense that in this arena, too, all was about to change. If you looked hard enough, listened closely enough, of course it was. But few were paying that kind of attention.

To her great credit, back at home Mum could not see what the fuss was about: she was a supporter of gay rights long before it was a fashionable cause, even among the hippie friends she had adopted. When I came home from school full of stories of how David was treated and the names he was called, she chided gently, 'Why don't you say something to the teachers?'

'I think David is being bullied because people say he is homosexual and I wonder if you might intervene.' That would have been the line. But God knows what the response would have been. Perhaps braver boys than I actually did bring it up, though I doubt it. The persecution of David was a feature of Sidcot, not an isolated case of injustice. The staff would have done nothing. We had ways of doing things, a code, a modus vivendi. And David's level in life had been found.

None of this is particularly unusual for a boarding school of that era – today we are well aware of worse, of teachers prosecuted finally for unspeakable depravity. Sidcot had a rugby coach in much more recent times who abused a child and was caught and sent to prison. The school said it had done all that could be expected to keep children safe. I am sure that's true. Nowadays schools fight a daily battle to keep children safe. There is no room for laxness, particularly in a boarding school.

In those days, well . . . it was optional, this battle. And Sidcot had no interest in fighting it. The school was conventionally cruel, conventionally abusive; it made no effort to be Quakerly. It was not a place of kindness and inclusivity. It was, for the vulnerable, a hellhole. Yes, they took a proportion of children who had been expelled from all other schools, who were lost, who had been given up on by everyone else. But when some of them turned out to be psychopaths in short trousers they had no further interest in helping out. Perhaps they thought the fresh air of the Mendips would be enough.

The whole structure of modern teaching practice when it came to vulnerable kids was never really thought of. We were simply thrown together. Some of us were abandoned by poor parents in nearby Bristol, others (more of them, I think) abandoned by feckless wealthy parents working abroad for some arm of the British government. A lot of distress in a small space. Some sank, some swam. We all swallowed a good deal of water in the process.

~

I arrived at Sidcot in September 1972. My preparation for school had been wholly inadequate, though I am not sure any amount of prior effort would have made it any more bearable. Mum and I had read Anthony Buckeridge's Jennings stories of pillow fights and stern but kindly masters; of the hero's wizard wheezes with his best friend, Darbishire. When things go wrong there's a 'Jumbo jet of a hoo-hah' and then all is well. It was alluring. But for all the Jennings bravado, I didn't, when it came to it, want to go.

The journey there from Bath was no more than forty minutes. Yet I wondered if it might go on for ever, that meandering drive through villages, past farms, out on to the busy A38. Perhaps we might break down and go home and decide the whole thing was a mistake. But the Hillman did the job. First days in boarding school are only sad for parents as they consider, if they have souls, the enormity of what they have done. For the children there is too much to take in for sadness to descend. Mum was brisk and to the point: 'You'll love it.'

Mum definitely saw Sidcot as that truck on to which her baby was being thrown, the escape from the burning village, the despairing leap of faith that consigned all she cared about to the truck and its drivers. She had faith in them; she seemed to think Anthony Buckeridge knew what he was talking about. She didn't realize that the drivers of this truck were drunk and the cargo dangerous.

Charles waited in the car. The teachers were full of false bonhomie – 'Hello, young man!' – as if it were all going to be tremendous fun.

I hung on to my radio. Once the jolly goodbyes were completed we were handed over to the fourth-formers to be shown the ropes: the changing rooms where we would be bullied, the dorms where we would try to sleep. We were also informed of our collective nickname as third-formers (the first year of the school began with the third form, for reasons lost in history).

We were Turds. This play on words was also a handy summary of our position in the school. We progressed from 'Hello, young man!' to 'Get in the shower, Turds' in a matter of hours. On the first full day of school, at the form meeting, the teacher gave us new boys our first warning, not about bullying but about snitching if you were bullied. 'Don't come running to me,' he said, 'if you get hit as a result of being cheeky.' It was a standing joke. 'Are you being cheeky?' a fifteen-year-old would ask an eleven-year-old, before punching him, with impunity, in the face.

One day we too would be able to bully the teary new boys. That was the implicit promise. But until that day came there was no remedy for being young, bruised, lost and far from home.

Every letter I wrote, every week without fail, from September 1972 to July 1979, my mother kept. I found them in her attic after she died. Each one was marked with the date it was read and bundled neatly with a single rubber band. The envelopes, in handwriting at first tentative, later wilder and less readable, addressed always to Mr and Mrs H. T. C. Webb. Hugh Thomas Charles, my stepfather's full name. Mum must have told me that that was how envelopes were properly addressed, even in these circumstances. Class, breeding, envelope etiquette. Our guard never let down. Mr and Mrs followed by the man's Christian name. Or, if it was just to a man, the name alone, followed by Esq. In that instance, Mr was only for business letters so would be wrong, a faux pas. My letters were free of faux pas. The missives, folded into little squares, always began 'Dear Mum and Dad' but were aimed entirely at Mum, except for the bit towards the end when I would enquire, as one does out of the customary politeness, about Charles's health. And then, heartfelt and unmannered, genuine, as so little else in life was, 'Luv to Gran and Guinea!'

The closest I ever got to full truth-telling in those early years was in my very first letter home, in which I announced: 'I have got to write to you every Sunday. I wonder what you are doing now.' And, in a slightly passive-aggressive tone at the end, 'I am glad Mrs Bamford gave me some sweets cos everybody else had lots and lots. We needn't have worried about me coming out for a month. Everybody's going out this weekend. Luv to Gran and Guinea.'

We needn't have worried. What a line! Who was 'we'? I was co-opted young into a world of 'sensible' decisions made by Mum. To rebel would have been unthinkable.

A few months later, perhaps following some anguished discussions with the housemaster: 'Please don't bother to come on Saturday cos there's no need. How's Charles. Hope he's well. Luv to Gran. Hope the [Quaker] Meeting's going well.'

And so we all got on with it.

You had seconds to make your mark. Perhaps days, but not much more than that. Thereafter the names, the reputations, would follow you to the age of eighteen, or until you gave up the ghost and left early. Lugs had big ears. Balls had big balls. Chin Choi Lau was renamed Bert because someone thought it funny. Feelers was a teacher who cupped the breasts of girls in his hands when they were queueing for dinner.

Or perhaps he'd only done it once. There was no statute of limitations at Sidcot. It's like the old joke about a man in a bar who sees someone looking forlorn and lonely in a corner. 'Who's that?' he asks his companion.

'Ah, that's Stealing Joe. He was a fireman who rescued a lot of people from a burning building. Then he became a tennis player and won Wimbledon. After that he invented a cure for a terrible disease and was awarded the Nobel Prize.'

'I don't get it. Why is he called Stealing Joe?'

'Well, you steal one apple . . .'

I avoided stealing an apple or anything else that might get me into serious long-term trouble.

It was not home but, in some ways, on Saturday nights, school managed to be, maybe for just an hour or so, more homely. It was nice to watch television sometimes without all the rigours, the unspoken stipulations, of TV-watching back in Bath, with those chairs turned round and the set having to be plugged in. We would be told to put on our dressing gowns and trooped into the sitting room of the master who ran the house where the younger boys lived. *Whatever Happened to the Likely Lads?* sticks in the mind: a class comedy, a remake of *The Likely Lads* which, in the black-and-white 1960s, had been one of television's early light-entertainment hits. The sequel was darker, fittingly so: the two pals had grown up and one of them was striving to be middle class, to escape from his roots. I don't remember laughing much. When I look at that housemaster's sitting room now, from above, from the vantage point of modernity, of child-centred education, of having kids of my own, I weep for us all. To send a child to live away from home at the age of eleven may be forgivable in some circumstances, but not in most. To send a child forty minutes down the road to the Sidcot of the 1970s was – sorry, Mum – a crime.

By the end of the first year, as the nation tried tinselly glamour in the first of many vain efforts to pull itself out of its slough of despond – as Slade sang 'Cum On Feel the Noize' – life at Sidcot was tolerable. I was large and could play rugby. (Letter home: 'I am in the scrum. I am bruised.') I could write essays. (Letter home: 'English is very disappointing: they give us boring books and ask us the maddest questions about them.') I was unhappy but also very good at hiding it: I was a dissembler. I could hunt with the hounds and run with the hare. My first report said as much. Mum explained the phrase to me. It seemed less of a reproach, more of a description of how to survive.

Visiting was discouraged. Mum came once in that first year and we went by bus to Weston-super-Mare. A whole Saturday afternoon away from it all. We ate in a café and clambered about on the rocks in bright sunshine. We pretended we were gazelles. But it was the rocks that gave me comfort. Rocks survive for centuries, for millennia. Rocks will last any course. They were hot in the sun, impassive. They could take any punishment. We had a hug at the end of the day and she agreed to write to the headmaster about the quality of the sausages we were served in the mornings. They were a proxy for quite a lot, but we left it at that.

How to survive. It was occasionally, sporadically Dickensian. Even for those of us who had avoided being at the bottom of the social scale. Every edge was hard. Every room echoed. Every floor hurt if you were hurled on to it. Doors clattered and slammed. A fashion at the time was shoes that clicked. You stuck little metal crescents on to the bottom of them – 'Blakey's shoe protectors', designed originally to make the heels last longer. At school they were used for their noise value: they created a mass panic of clicks when large numbers of us were in the corridors. Screams and clicks and manic laughter. And in the rooms off the corridors, anything went. In the showers, cornered by older boys, you would be punched by one, manhandled on to the next to be punched again, handed back. On and on until the tears came. Nothing could stop this happening. 'I want you in the changing rooms now' was a phrase you came to dread. You had to go. There was no appeal to be made to the teachers, no authority that could protect younger or vulnerable boys. On a grand baroque scale, the Quakers who ran Sidcot – the board of governors, the headmaster, the senior teachers, all of them – abrogated responsibility. They knew but they didn't care.

Just occasionally they were forced to intervene, when the level of violence really got out of hand. In my first year at the school one boy broke his knuckles on another. We were eleven.

The second year was probably the worst. In the outside world the IRA were beginning their mainland campaign, there were colliery disasters, the oil shock and the threat of petrol rationing, and a serial arsonist called Peter Dinsdale, 'Daft Peter', began to set fires in houses in the north-east of England that would result in twenty-six deaths. Never mind Slade and glam rock: the real Britain that people lived in was a place of coal dust-coughing despair, of violence in place of politics; of men with matches in their hands and madness in their eyes.

Sidcot caught the mood. The fourth-form dormitory was above the dining room. It was huge, with sixty steel beds. There was a matron – enormously fat – who would sniff our underwear to check its freshness and confiscate pornographic magazines, which she would keep in a pile in the laundry room. A master was nominally in charge but at night he would stay in his flat watching films on a black-and-white TV. The Lower Fourth had the south side, the Upper Fourth the north. In the lower form we were easy pickings. Our beds were turned upside down. Pillows were held over heads. And, after fitful sleep, the awakening bell would be rung in your ear by a sadist.

I protected my radio, though, and smuggled it into my bed. At night, as the sounds of mayhem reduced, giggles and farts replacing thuds and cries, I would press my ear against the speaker and listen to Douglas Stuart presenting *The World Tonight* on Radio 4. The two elections of 1974, a national nervous breakdown, a giddy time of tension and uncertainty: to me the whole thing was balm. I was soothed by Douglas Stuart's voice whispering out of my ITT Tiny Super and the knowledge that, elsewhere in the country, issues were being faced that seemed relatively minor compared with the horrors we faced each night at school. 'Who runs the country?' asked Ted Heath. A deliciously large question posed by a large man with a big car. A much better question than 'Who's going to kill the Turds?' Douglas Stuart allowed a sense of perspective that made life more bearable, more manageable. It says something about Sidcot that the outside world, in the mid-1970s, of all times, seemed gentler, more civilized. I think it helped that the rest of the nation was so troubled: it suggested to me that trouble was normal, dysfunction was normal, even violence was OK. We were a proper microcosm, a proper specimen of the age. I never felt Sidcot was out of place, that my experience was unfair or unjust. Nobody was having much of a time of it, or so it seemed.

The boys' lavatories at Sidcot would have disgraced a prison. They were one of the most disgusting, unsanitary places I have been and, in later life, in Russia, in the Middle East, in the heart of Africa, I have been in a few. They were properly subterranean. To reach them you had to go downstairs and through a tunnel. They were unheated. In the winter they would freeze. The water in the lavatory pans would have a sheen of ice in the mornings. They stank, mainly of the ammonia with which they were sprayed every day. But of cigarette smoke, too, because, being so uniquely disgusting, few members of staff would ever venture there. They were the scene of epic bullying. Doors were kicked in. Boys were held down, half-drowned in muck. With the cubicles open at the top and bottom, there was no privacy, no refuge. On the backs of the doors people carved their names, often with dates. It struck me that the dates, just as in prison, really mattered. I was here. On this day. I want you to know that I was alive, then. I had a soul even if it was being crushed.

To the showers and the cockroaches. They scuttled when we went in but they jointly owned the place with the bullies and their defiant presence was a part of life. Lighter-fuel executions helped keep their numbers down but no further effort was made. It fascinated me that their bodies seemed to disappear, as if evaporating rather than burning. This was the only science knowledge I possessed when I left the school.

Lord Carrington, the patrician foreign secretary in Margaret Thatcher's first government, used to defend his lopsided education by saying that he had gone to school 'before science was invented'. It had been invented by the time I went to Sidcot but it was not taken seriously. You did not have to do it. And I did not. I didn't show any interest in it and the teachers had none in me. So, in the year before O-Levels (the equivalent of modern-day GCSEs), I stopped going to physics and chemistry. I would not take the exams and nobody cared. Since I had already, as mentioned previously, been banned from biology, it meant that I would leave what looked to the outside world like a fee-paying school awash with privilege without being asked to attempt to gain a single science qualification. Nobody batted an eyelid. Nobody sat down with me and explained that science might matter. Nobody rang to discuss it with my mother. This was the age of *Tomorrow's World* on the BBC: chaps in ill-fitting suits explaining new-fangled devices called computers that could remember things and work out our sums while they whirred and clicked. Science, and in particular technology, was on the cusp of something big. In our corner of the Mendips, nobody had noticed.

The truth was that Sidcot was collapsing, like the nation. It had lost its bearings. And, as well as science, we had lost touch with humanity. For all the talk in Meeting about the spiritual world, there was no attention at all given to the mental well-being of the children trapped there. We were not expected to have inner lives. We were not allowed to be unhappy. It was against the rules. It was around half-way through my time at the school when my much-loved granny died, in the middle of a term. I would have been thirteen or fourteen. What did the school know about my life? Perhaps much less than would be the case today: Mum was not exactly open. But the death of a grand-mother is surely worth some kind of effort being expended, some kind of pastoral check being made? None was. We were sitting in the common room, playing a song called 'Ripples' by Genesis, when a master came in. 'Webb, would you call home, please?'

This was unusual. The school had one telephone box, from which all live contact with the outside world was conducted. You had to queue. People came out grinning or sobbing or deep in thought, or often just disappointed that efforts to reverse the charges had failed or they had run out of two-pence pieces to keep the phone fed. Older children would sometimes throw out younger ones in mid-sentence.

On this occasion there was no one there. I dialled home and Mum said: 'Granny has died, I'm afraid.'

And then, a little too quickly, 'Are you OK to carry on?'

Carry on with what? It was my first death. Coming from where I came from, lonely as I was, tied to Mum with such powerful threads as I was, it felt as if it brought her own end closer. Might she be next, and soon? And what of Granny herself, a woman I didn't really know but loved all the same? The finality of death is not one single shock, is it? It comes as a multiplicity of shocks, wave upon wave. Can you not show them that page? Will they not walk through snow to the door? What will happen to the medicine bottles from which she drank the sweet wine in the Wimpy Bar? What about her hands, that skin around her knuckles that you could pick away from the bone and squeeze between your fingers?

I said I was fine. I went back to the common room and then to prep, which was held in a large classroom in the modern block. I told no one. But that night I had an English essay to write and I composed a long, angry attack on everything and everyone and a homage to Granny and a lament about life and its futility.

It came back with a tick and a relatively high mark. But, face to face, eye to eye, heart to heart, nobody ever mentioned it. Perhaps Mum, when she rang the school, had not gone into detail. Given the cost of phone calls in those days, you didn't dawdle over them. But even if she hadn't mentioned it, might a master not have thought to ask? Probably better to let it blow over, would have been the thinking. Not much to be done. It was not unusual to hear children crying in the night at Sidcot. What would have been unusual would have been for anyone to do anything about it.

We lived on a diet of table tennis and cigarettes, which we smoked with impunity in the woods around the school. We would take packets of ten Player's No. 6 up to the combe, the little copse that overlooked the valley. That was Saturday afternoon. Gossip and fags.

The combe. During the war a tougher, perhaps a more thoughtful generation of Sidcot kids had come up here to pick up incendiary bombs dropped in error by German planes searching for Bristol, ten miles to the north. There are stories in school histories of the bombs being smuggled into school and decommissioned by plucky pupils. Stories of the glow they could see from the woods at night when Bristol was ablaze.

Only thirty years separated us from them.

On Saturday evenings, the older children were allowed

to have discos in the girls' shed, that neat and nice-smelling alternative to the boys', with its polished floors and clean walls. It wasn't exactly a disco. The boys had to ask the girls to dance. We would gyrate, in half-light, to 'Freebird' or 'The Jean Genie': 'Sits like a man but he smiles like a reptile . . .'

Older, more confident couples would snog. Some may have gone further, though sexual shame, particularly for girls, was a big dampener. There was no real sex.

In any case, we were often too drunk. This was courtesy of the local cider farm, which would sell its disgusting scrumpy to children, apparently free of any sanction from school or police. A gallon was 70p. The patches of sick, in acid greens and yellows, would stain the flowerbeds in front of the main building. Dances would sometimes be called off even before 'Freebird' was played because everyone seemed to be vomiting. Fourteen-year-olds would be put in the showers to try to bring them round before the staff found them. People would be carried to bed. When we were older, fifteen or sixteen would do, we would go to the local village pubs on Saturdays and hang out in the saloon bars. Only when the numbers got too great, the chatter of young voices too obviously out of kilter with the law of the land, would the barman chuck us out.

When the dances went ahead everyone would be deafened. That was important. For this purpose, Black Sabbath was our band. Yes or Emerson, Lake & Palmer for the pseudo-thoughtful ones who liked wordy, pretentious silliness, but mostly it was the loud, frenzied sounds of Free, Deep Purple, Led Zeppelin or Quo. Music that screamed and clattered and revved and destroyed. And melancholia by the bucketful. God, we loved that maudlin stuff: babe I gotta leave you, time's passing, love's lost (again). In the small society of our school, we listened to the music of ersatz despair, of self-indulgence. In the early days, before they were snuffed out by the harsh realities of the 1970s, psychedelic rockers played with our minds. The Crazy World of Arthur Brown were a personal favourite, as was 'Fire', Arthur Brown's signature song ('I am the god of hellfire!').

On record-players around the school, in form rooms and sixth-form studies, the sounds of catastrophe would echo. We even had a school band for a time – we had the clothes, the look, the hair, though not the talent. We pretended to be Led Zeppelin, singing 'Stairway to Heaven':

> In a tree by the brook
> There's a songbird who sings
> Sometimes all of our thoughts are misgiven.

What kind of inane nonsense was this? Hard rock clashed in me with a core part of my identity. I was a rocker but I was a language pedant, verging, let's be frank, on language prig. I liked words. I could weigh them, play with them, use them. These dimwit singers mainly could not. 'All of our thoughts are misgiven.' Seriously.

We revelled in the nonsense, though; drank deeply from Free's wishing well. Remember, there was nothing to do in those days. Really, nothing. If you weren't kicking a ball around or reading a book or snogging in the tunnel that linked the boys' and girls' sides of the school, you actually had no occupation. Into this void came the radio, for me, but louder, much louder, came Zeppelin. We would sit around, in downtime between lessons and tea or tea and prep, destroying our ears. It was the era of Dolby Stereo. Snobbishness and nerdiness about sound were taking off but, more than anything else, we wanted volume. If you weren't Dazed and Confused, you weren't doing it right.

Why were the girls at Sidcot treated so differently from the boys? We never saw it as odd. Girls were a separate species. They were expected to giggle and waft and go into nursing. On their side of the school, they were given comfy rooms to sleep in, soft furnishings, pastel-coloured walls. Pretty things for the pretty section of the human race. So yes, it was a mixed school, and that suggests a progressive, modern approach. But the reality was a kind of apartheid, physically and mentally. And although the girls were not bullied, they were not exactly treated as equals, either, in the official, Quaker-approved manner. Their sport was netball: we thought that a joke. Their concentration in lessons, all that writing stuff down: equally risible. The ones who didn't let you 'feel them up', to use the unwoke jargon of the day: stuck up and frigid. The ones who did: whores.

Girls 'let you do things'. Or didn't. They had no agency.

What they might want never concerned anyone. Even the female staff were underlings. We called the men 'sir' but the women by their first names. This is not just strange, it is fundamentally unQuakerly, since equality is one of the central tenets of Quakerism. The Society of Friends was, as a sect, way ahead of the game when it came to feminism. But in the schools they ran? They couldn't summon up the courage of their convictions.

I did, in a small way, break this sexist mould. Useless at woodwork, thrown out of all the sciences, searching for subjects to study for O-Level, I enrolled in the cookery classes. This was not, however, a political statement. I was not interested in cooking. I did not believe that cookery was for boys as much as for girls. I just had nothing else to do. The teacher, Dorothy Powell, Dottie to us, thought it was a bit silly and possibly unnatural. She had never had a boy in her class and probably didn't really want one, particularly one who was likely to be trouble. But she was a warm and inclusive woman and she was persuaded to allow it. And so it came to pass that I began weekly cookery classes.

In a school that was so sparsely appointed, the cookery block was quite a revelation. Each of us had our own tiny kitchen. Ingredients were supplied. 'Set the oven to hot!' decreed Dottie Powell at the start of every lesson. As for academic or practical success, well, we learned to 'fold' lighter flour into a heavier mix with the back of a spoon. We made bread, and threw the dough at the walls outside, where it stuck, satisfyingly, for the rest of my school-days. We learned to produce dishes for every occasion. White fish with mashed potato for a patient convalescing after a stay in hospital. A hearty picnic. Stew.

What was I doing? Insolent and foolish, uninterested in cooking and unable to do anything else. Taking the indulgence of a very decent teacher for granted. I did not complete the O-Level in the end. Again, nobody cared. Least of all me.

Quakers have never excelled at sport. No battles were won on the playing fields of Sidcot but plenty of small-scale violent skirmishes took place there, on Wednesdays, at a safe distance from the peace and talk of peace at Sunday Meeting. I can't imagine in the modern era that compulsory violent games are part of the curriculum at Sidcot or any other Quaker school, but at that time they certainly were. We were hardened in the gym. Actually, before gym, at kit inspection, lined up against the wall. Every shape of boy: fatties like me, emaciated figures with vests that hung off their shoulders; one or two properly athletic types. Prior to any kind of activity, everyone had to be inspected. Anything missing, any piece of kit out of place, any gym shoe less than fully white earned you a whack on the bum from Mr Sisman, who ran the boys' sport at Sidcot for all my time there and serves as an exemplar of all that was maladjusted about the school in the early 1970s and all that was improving about the school, about the decade, towards its end. Mr Sisman was a sports master out of central casting. A neat little man with sandy hair and an air of barely suppressed violence, always dressed in a tracksuit except on Sundays, when he would appear around the school in natty slacks and a blazer. You never quite knew when he might hit you. Or frown as if he was readying his hitting arm, then smile and let you off.

He was a believer in the kind of mass punishments commonly meted out to prisoners. The wallop with a gym shoe for everybody if one boy's kit was not properly adjusted. An entire dormitory slippered because two people were fighting after lights out.

His party piece was a game in which medicine balls – those heavy, weighted balls people use for exercise – were placed in the centre of the gym and all of us gathered round them in a circle in small teams. The aim was to get as many of the balls as you could into your team space using any means at your disposal. A whistle blew and mayhem began: heads cracked, arms flailed, mouths were bloodied. The useless boys held back and were abused by all. The game favoured the strong, the violent, the reckless.

That was the warm-up. A walk that must have been a kind of prison march for the smaller, weaker boys took us over that footbridge across the A38 down to the sports field, where there were two rugby pitches. We wore shorts and cotton shirts and carried our boots, in rain and snow, in gales. We stood shivering while teams were picked. The same boys at the top of the list and the same at the bottom every time. And the same fate for those who hated all of this. Why didn't their parents complain? Why didn't the teachers recognize that rugby was not for all? Nobody would have dreamed of it then. You just had to get on with it.

I was not exactly a top player but I was good enough for a new level of recklessness Mr Sisman decided to introduce: to toughen up his boys by sending them to the local village rugby club, where he had friends who still played. Two of us were sent to Winscombe RFU one Saturday, with the instruction to fit in and do as we were told. We were picked up at the front of the school by a man in an elderly Land Rover. There were no seats in the back – 'Just hang on, it's not far.' We were probably sixteen, still growing, still soft-boned. Winscombe RFU's third team, to which we had been gifted, was a collection of local farmers and publicans, some of whom seemed to be in their fifties. They looked us up and down and told us to mind our opponents, Yatton Thirds, who could be 'punchy bastards'.

We played on a field recently inhabited by cows. Nobody could catch the ball. But nobody minded. The game was a blur of the pain caused when large men crush soft-boned boys. My pal, as well as being much better than me, played in the relative safety out on the wing, where he stood a chance of survival and might even manage to evade tacklers and run for his life. I played in the scrum, the danger zone, the territory in amateur rugby where anything goes.

They had told me to play prop, the position at the front of the scrum where you have to grapple with the opposition. In set scrums the entire weight of both packs goes through you. One of the first things I discovered that day is that grown men have very hard heads. In the first ruck, as I tentatively inserted myself and pushed, several of the opposing team used their shaven skulls as weapons of war. It helped that they had no necks. Their brains were effectively encased in upturned, skin-covered buckets, sculpted to vaguely human form, which could be employed to wound and stun. I was seriously concerned for my soft nose, my still-pink ears.

The opposing prop, a man in his forties wider than he was tall, had elected not to shave and rubbed his chin with huge enthusiasm against my ear. Not getting much of a reaction, at the second scrum he freed his arm and punched me, playfully, for a Yatton man, just above the eye, hard enough to draw blood.

At half-time, as the chaps drank beer out of a watering can and picked the cow dung off their boots, I tried to stop the blood from trickling into my eyes. There were no substitutes in rugby in those days: you had to stay on the field unless you were injured so badly that you couldn't carry on. About midway through the second half I was taken off, never to return.

What were they thinking? The school, Mr Sisman, the team? Nowadays Winscombe RFU has a child-protection officer and a ladies team. They are paragons of responsibility. I am sure the good men of Yatton, then and now, are hard but fair and would not want to bully schoolboys. My opposite number would not have thought himself a monster in the 1970s and he wasn't, by the standards of the time. At the end of the game he came over, shook my hand and said, 'Thank you, prop.'

It was the first time a man had hit me and the first time a man had treated me as an equal, a player, a person. Perhaps Mr Sisman was on to something.

I know Mr Sisman continues to be regarded with affection by many. I bear him no ill will, in fact rather the opposite. He was in parts cruel and in parts a gruff but genuinely caring human being. Perhaps we all were. Once, in a basketball game, I stopped one of the much-bullied boys from shooting a hoop. It wasn't difficult: I just towered above him and put a hand in the way. Mr Sisman glowered at me. 'Why do that?' He was at least sporadically aware of a better way of conducting ourselves. The incident was over in seconds but I have never forgotten it. I was lucky enough to be a favourite. I think he felt sorry for me, or at least that I might redeem myself, or perhaps find myself, on the rugby field. And, for all his faults, I think he was right. There was redemption in the mud.

Or on the way to Twickenham, the home of the England team. The school, caught in the uncomfortable terrain between old-fashioned public-school traditions and the Quaker way, used to send the first XV to see England play. It was one of a very few school trips, hugely sought-after, not least because we could each take a girl. The lucky girls were loaded on to a coach, which deposited us at the ground in west London. In those days you stood. Or tried to. It was chaotic. Though not as chaotic as the journey

home, which would be broken in the town of Marlbor-
ough at around pub closing time. Chips in the high street.
Booze smuggled back on to the bus. Girls and boys on a
once-a-year outing. What could possibly go wrong? We
always made it home but it felt as if some kind of emergency pressure valve was being opened. Nothing felt stable
or explicable; nothing quite fitted into a bigger picture.

We were too poorly educated to know this, but our
school displayed the kind of decay that a way of life gov-
erned by Romanticism can bring. In place of authority
and duty (boring, boring, boring), you go for passion. Sex
'n' drugs 'n' rock 'n' roll. Liberate your inner self. Be true to
your spirit. It had been a decade since Philip Larkin had
lamented that sex was 'a wrangle for the ring'. In that time
so much had changed. We were free, at least in theory.
We were encouraged to do what felt right, to value pleasure for its own sake, the moment, the urge: 'I took her
home, to my place, watchin' every move on her face . . .'

There was a coffee bar, staffed by pupils, open at lunchtime and in the evenings. It sold Coke, Mars bars, sherbet
dips and violently colourful sweets. In those days, health
food was still a minority pursuit, most of its dishes of
interest mainly to rabbits or commune-dwellers, and it
was unheard of at school. Well, almost: it was rumoured
that there had been a petition in the 1960s to improve the
food. Apparently, the petitioners had been punished, even
when they provided evidence of vitamin C deficiency. The
school proudly grew its own vegetables in gardens that

spread out in front of the grand steps where the headmaster had his study. Proudly grew them and then murdered them in kitchens that stank of veggie death: boiling that began every morning and seemed to go on all day. Meals were designed to fill, not to nourish. And, having filled our stomachs, we would go to the coffee bar to rot our teeth. The mass damage that must have been done there without anyone batting an eyelid.

The idea was that the coffee bar would be a social hub, a place for bubbly conversation in the lull between lunch and afternoon lessons. Furnished with banquettes upholstered in red plastic, Formica tables and hard chairs that scraped across the linoleum floor, it was designed to be used, evacuated and quickly cleaned. That responsibility the school took seriously. But when there were people in it nobody policed it. In my time it was the scene of mafia-style corruption. Multiple scams were controlled by the hardest, the most ruthless. Those of us who served there, handing out Refreshers to fourth-formers, would take the money and keep it, or give it to our mates to be re-spent. Or we would just eat the stock. At the very least we operated on a 'sell one, gift one, steal one' basis.

The coffee-bar store room had a counter which opened on to the main room. On some days, when the moon was high and full, toast would be ordered so that the junior person on serving duty had to go out the back to the toaster. Arms would be thrust over the counter and indiscriminate hands simply grabbed as much stock as could be stuffed into mouths. Even when it was closed the theft carried on: senior boys with a talent for woodwork fashioned spears out of broomsticks and compasses to impale chocolate bars and pull them through the metal grilles of the shutters. The music master, who nominally ran the whole enterprise, must have seen all of this and not cared or not known how to stop it. Or perhaps there was some kind of Quaker lesson about the downside of commerce that we were meant to be imbibing. All property is theft? Whatever the truth, the fault was not really his, but ours.

Some of our number became master shoplifters. A few boys, dissatisfied with the pickings on offer in the coffee bar, went further afield. Two of them had persuaded the matron who kept the pornography that it would be handy to have special pockets sewn inside their jackets for the safekeeping of personal items. These they used to store their booty on thieving expeditions to local shops. Several semi-successful criminal careers were begun in the coffee bar. The school formally celebrated those Old Scholars who went on to a lifetime of overseeing irrigation schemes in dusty, fly-blown places, but the felons were the ones who could truly claim that Sidcot made them, or at least assisted them in honing their skills. Two boys known to me went into cocaine smuggling; one is rumoured to have spent time in an Australian jail. Nothing he did to get himself there, nothing he saw along the way, none of the social mores he ignored, the upset he caused, the cunning he deployed, can be separated from that coffee bar in the Mendips.

The coffee bar was the school in microcosm – ineptly run, corrupt, out of control. Deep Purple screaming in the corner about freedom or eternity or love. In the foam-and-plastic banquettes, we nodded our heads to the beat and feasted on stolen Curly Wurlies.

We were potent, we were freshly untroubled by our inhibitions. As we grew through the school, victims becoming victimizers, we felt ourselves to be on fire. In our little corner we were not troubled by conventions, or so we thought. Of course, in reality we were horribly keen to enforce those conventions that mattered to us, and enforce them we did, with the vigour that Romantics always seize for themselves: 1789! To the barricades! Like French Revolutionaries, we rushed about with our hair getting longer and our self-belief ever huger. And, as in the Revolution, the guillotine was much-used.

Casualties like David, the boy accused of homosexuality, would pass through the school unnoticed at best, unhelped by the defiant guitar riffs of our long-haired heroes. Free love did not extend to David. No aspect of freedom touched his life. Nobody at the coffee bar would have served him, still less given him a free drink.

Even our successes at Sidcot seemed somehow hobbled by the stench of the place, the suffering imposed on us and imposed by us on each other. Every year, at the end of the summer term, in the heady days in which the long break beckoned and school seemed at its most benign, there would be a speech competition, customarily entered by a handful of sixth-formers. Parents were invited and big cars would crunch on newly combed gravel in the car park for hours before the event. Parents, broken, grotesque, greying versions of ourselves ('Jesus, have you *seen* Thompson's mother?'), would bend and stretch and make their way, via the drinks table, to the big hall. We saw few strangers during term-time and it felt special. There were a lot of eyes on the competitors.

I decided I wanted to enter. I was fourteen. Only in the Lower Fifth. Nobody so young had ever put their name forward. But I wanted to do it and I wanted to win. I wanted people to applaud. I wanted everyone to notice me. 'Wouldn't you be nervous?' friends asked. God, I was nervous. More than nervous. Properly terrified of the void that sucks into its depths those who are not noticed. Not being famous: that was the horror.

I worked hard on my speech and wrote it out in full. 'The Evils of Capitalism' was its title. A book in the library about the behaviour of multinationals (then a big deal on the left) was the source. But the swagger was mine. The looks up from the lectern. The humour. The grand theatrical turns to the headmaster with rhetorical questions that caused his rictus smile to take on a life of its own, to eat his own mouth. Screw him: I was on fire.

There was a break for the judges to consider their

verdict. I can still, forty-five years later, feel the eyes of the parents on me as I walked across the grass to return to the hall. Mum, I am in charge here. I am bossing it. I am a person standing out from the crowd.

We trooped back in, the gentle hubbub hushed as the dignitaries took their seats, the local worthies brought in to be judges. To decide my future. A pause and a rustling of paper and a bit of chat about the importance of doing one's best and how everyone had. Then the announcements. The runner-up: not me. Time for the composed face, the kind of face you practise in TV for the shots they call 'cutaways' or 'noddies', in which you fake interest, or surprise, or anything. The face you see on Hollywood stars at the Oscars as the winner's name is read out. This mattered more than the Oscars to me: the youngest-ever winner of the Dymond Speech competition. The older kids I'd beaten looked a bit shell-shocked but I was gracious in victory. I got a book token and a taste, just a taste, of a hallucinatory drug. I felt like a cross between Laurence Olivier and JFK. I could turn heads. I could make the weather.

It was ludicrous. This was no triumph. There was nothing, no one to triumph over. The school was almost devoid of any dramatic or artistic talent. I may have been better than the others – by a country mile – but I was useless. Naïve, unread, uneducated and unfunny. I think I knew this. I think, deep down, part of the thrill was in not being found out. Perhaps it always has been. Who knew where anything was heading? The best way of surviving was to invent a reality, a story, and stick to it. In shifting times there are opportunities if you can grasp them. This Quaker maelstrom had its moments of possibility, of promise.

6

Immoral Tales

In April 1978, a year before A-Levels, three of us who scanned the *Guardian* every day in our newspaper reading room asked for permission to go to London to take part in a march and music festival organized by the Anti-Nazi League, a front for the Socialist Workers Party. Like boarding-school revolutionaries through history, we were drawn to the red flags. I am not sure I could actually think of myself as 'working class' owing to, well, Mum, but the idea of taking part in a mass struggle against evil was enormously appealing, as seen from our dull corner of the Mendips, unnoticed by history, untouched by momentous events. We were encouraged at Sidcot to be in the vanguard of the politics of Quakerism even as we practised hate at home. That politics veered towards the left, without the kindness that concern for one's fellow humans might suggest. It was not hugely thought through. But we believed we were in the right and that mattered a lot.

The other advantage of a trip to London was that we could go to a pornographic film in Soho. It was the perfect elision of lust and goodness, truth and pleasure. Romanticism in action: Rousseau would have approved. The school examined the first part of our suggested programme and didn't have the capacity to imagine the second. Permission was granted and the three of us were allowed to go by rail to London with the proviso that we stayed with the parents of one of the boys, who lived in Surbiton, a short train ride home from central London.

What a glorious day it was. We went dressed like extras in *Withnail and I* and marched in Trafalgar Square next to girls with no bras. We waved placards declaring 'NO IMMI-GRATION CONTROLS'. We went to the park in Hackney and pretended to enjoy horribly distorted music played by people who screamed rude things about the Queen. Then Chris, one of our number, already worried that the noise might make us deaf, had the courage to point out that some immigration controls were probably rather a good thing. His exact words (he was from Welsh farming stock) were: 'If you go to someone's house you should knock, and if they don't want you to come in, then you should leave.'

Ah. Perhaps we didn't belong in Hackney Park that day. We bailed out and went to Soho, where we saw a film called *Immoral Tales*, participating in a 1970s ritual as British and wholesome as a prawn cocktail in a power cut. We saw, for the first time, sex on screen, in the company of men in raincoats, some of whom moved suddenly and jerkily and left before the denouement. I am not sure the porn would have particularly upset the SWP, who turned out in later years to be no slouches when it came to sexual exploitation, but our next action was quite Romantic in satisfying hunger rather than principle.

A long-running strike at the Garners group of steak-houses over the issue of union rights was being enforced by pickets outside their Soho restaurant. It was a dismal scene, the pickets gloomy and silent, their placards alleging management crimes. We were left-wing, therefore we supported them. But there were free tables inside. What the hell. We sneaked in, averting our eyes from the glares of the pickets, and dined on melon boats with maraschino cherries, gammon steaks and Black Forest gâteau. Like all the best Romantics, we were not really political. We were hungry.

Later, at Victoria station, because we were also broke, having spent our cash on the meal and the film, we asked a man for money so that we could get to the parents in Surbiton. It never occurred to us that this was actually begging and nor, apparently, did it occur to the man. Like proper public schoolboys, we took his address and promised to pay him back but we never did, because we were also hippies. Our Quaker education had taught us to be free.

But as our hair grew, so did we. I had returned to the school in the autumn of 1977 ready for two more years of disorder. By now a few of the brighter parents, or those

who gave a damn, had cottoned on to the school's academic failings and half the year had been taken out and
sent to better schools ('OK, OK, we'll spend the money
now') or local state sixth-form colleges so that they could
actually learn something in an ambience of relative normality. This was a school tradition. One of Sidcot's most
celebrated alumni, the film producer Tim Bevan, who left
a couple of years after I arrived, speaks warmly of the
place – 'I learned tenacity, resilience and not necessarily
taking no for an answer' – but hopped it to Cheltenham
College for the sixth form. I wonder, if Tim had seen out
Sidcot, what he would be doing now. Taking the money at
the Weston-super-Mare Odeon?

Once Sidcot had sent someone to Oxford. He was said
to have gone on to read chemistry, which gave the lab and
Mr Hope a spurious glamour. But since that glorious day
no one had gone anywhere. Few went to any university.
Some lived locally in doss houses after leaving school.
Others (the more successful, or sophisticated) wandered
the world. My pal Adrian left for Morocco on the night
after his last O-Level.

For those of us left, it was decision time. We were senior
members of a tottering enterprise in a tottering world. In
South Africa Steve Biko had died in police custody. In
Europe bombs, often homemade, and bullets were flying –
leftists killing bankers, rightists killing union officials. And
Fleetwood Mac had just released *Rumours*.

That last event mattered a good deal, looking back. In

our sixth-form common room we were bewitched. Complex melodies, acoustic as well as electric guitar, a variety of voices and moods, songs of hope, songs of despair. And Stevie Nicks, with those big eyes, that throaty, drawly voice. I had come a long way from Shostakovich and even further from 'Smoke on the Water'. Embarrassingly, given how mushy much of it feels in retrospect, *Rumours* changed me. And it changed Sidcot.

As Fleetwood Mac sang: 'If there's been a fool around, it's got to be me.'

Rumours suggested a new and more complex world in which the things you do have consequences. In which pride can be allied with regret. It took its toll on the certainties that had shaped us up to then. It pointed me in a new direction. *Rumours* – and an interview with the new headmaster.

Thomas Leimdorfer did not impress us one bit when we first set eyes on him. Too small, too foreign. He had an eastern European accent. For all our professed Quaker internationalism, we were remarkably suspicious, hostile even, when faced with those who came from further afield than the West Country. We had developed a high-functioning xenophobia in which we could say all the right things about the wider world while despising it when it impinged on our lives.

We did not want our secrets discovered. We did not want Mr Leimdorfer to pry into the control exerted by the older children over the younger. The fact that the cider farm was happy to take our money and destroy our brain cells. The affairs between staff members that led to some refusing to speak to others but were a source of great amusement and ribaldry among the pupils. The affair between a sixth-former and a teacher. The corporal punishment, the general chaos. The boy who took another boy off to South Wales during term-time for reasons that were not clear.

And above all, the caving. When Thomas Leimdorfer learned that the grandly named Sidcot School Speleological Society was run entirely by boys, who would disappear down large and (sometimes even more terrifyingly) small holes in the ground on Saturday afternoons without anyone monitoring where they were or when they would be back, he was enough of a spoilsport to insist on adult involvement. A Sidcot tradition bit the dust.

Here's a challenge for you: choose one area where life has moved on from the 1970s with such completeness that the mind is utterly boggled. I am talking about attitudes, not technological advances: multi-channel TV doesn't count and neither does the internet. You might plump for environmental concern (we were still abandoning hedgerows and destroying woods and, of course, burning coal) or the end of the Cold War certainties in international life. Out of badness, as the Northern Irish say, I would add the improvement of Rugby Union when it became a professional game.

But surely top of the list should be the attitudinal change

to risk as it relates to children. We think of childhood being invented a century or so ago and of teenagers being fêted (or not) as a separate species some time after the Second World War. But what, then, should be done with them? How to approach the business of looking after kids of all ages in a new world where, in other spheres, 'Do what you want' was becoming the mantra? Could you 'do what you want' to, or with, kids? What rights did they have? When they transgressed, did you beat them or merely point out the error of their ways? Engage with them or crush them? Laugh at them or with them? Treat them as adults or cut them some slack? Sidcot tried all of the above, unable to decide what was right and what was wrong.

And this was particularly the case with risk. The rugby madness. The *Lord of the Flies* abandonment of those who could have done with some adult protection. And yes, the caving. I don't know anything about the modern iteration of my old school but I think we can safely assume that it is unlikely to be letting the kids go down caves at the weekend without knowing where they are. Nor will they be left exposed to predators, either the type of abusive adult about whom there has subsequently been so much publicity or exploitative fellow pupils. There were predatory children, too, about whom we hear much less because of course we were, in a sense, all at it. For every recently prosecuted 'evil prep-school monster' there were a thousand little monsters. It was the way life was. This is not to excuse it: far from it. But if you prosecuted all the hateful things done at just one Quaker school in the Mendips in the 1970s, the courts would buckle.

Thomas Leimdorfer, our new headmaster, intended no prosecutions. But he was a reformer. He had a modern grasp of safety, of responsibility, of community, that was indeed foreign: foreign to the school, foreign to us.

There's a moment in John Fowles' *Daniel Martin* when some apparently foppish postwar Oxford students find a body in the river. One of them, on being warned that it is 'a bloody awful sight', responds calmly: 'I landed at Anzio, old man.' Here is a strangeness that is an intrinsic element of the 1970s mix: there were plenty of people, often people in authority, who had personal histories that would blow the modern mind. Nowadays a politician with an arresting back story might have grown up in a council house or come to Britain as the child of poor immigrants. Minor-league disadvantage. In those properly screwed-up days we were all the children of stonking A-grade trauma. We were, although we only dimly understood it, within touching distance of dramas that had changed human history. Never mind the odd lockdown: these characters had personal experience of the cataclysmic spasms suffered by the whole world in the twentieth century. The dislocation of everything to the extent that nothing could or would be the same again. An end to everything. And a rebirth alongside the atom bomb, in the new and constant shadow of mass death.

Thomas Leimdorfer had not been on the beaches at

Anzio. Far worse: he was a Hungarian Jew whose wider family had been given up to the Nazis and the death camps. His grandparents were gone, his father too. And then, in 1956, at the age of fourteen, he had seen his country's freedom crushed by Soviet troops. He and his mother managed to escape from a new totalitarian nightmare, across a field to Austria and eventually to England, where Mr Leimdorfer became a Quaker and a teacher.

We knew none of this. An age away from social media, suffering – licking your wounds, rebuilding your life – was something you did alone, or in private with your family. Decent people did not emote. It was just over thirty years, a little chunk of a lifetime, since a German Panzer division had entered the French village of Oradour-sur-Glane and massacred almost all of the inhabitants, more than 600 men, women and children. We knew about what had happened at Oradour from *The World at War*, the documentary series narrated by Laurence Olivier, which we would gather to watch every week in a classroom set up with a TV. The opening scene of that story was the scorched, roofless remains of the buildings. Olivier delivered a single line that made the hairs stand up on the back of your neck: 'Nobody lives here now.'

We knew our history and our history, Europe's history, was fresh. But (how we have changed) it was bad form for public events to be mixed with private matters. I don't think Mr Leimdorfer's past was ever mentioned, or even considered particularly interesting.

Still, he made a difference. The exigencies of his life had turned him into a kindly, thoughtful man but a man of action, too. He was inheriting, at the age of thirty-five, a disaster zone and he was keen to sort out what could be saved and what could not.

It came as an early shock that among the things he thought could not be saved was me. He had done his research before our first meeting. He had looked at my reports and at my exam results.

'You are doing too many A-Levels,' he said. 'Just take two and try your best.' Two! This was the route that led to a polytechnic, at best. It was the second-class option. The working-class option, as Mum might have put it. I think I cried out, 'No!'

On paper, he was dead right. I had scraped a handful of O-Levels but had failed maths and had not taken any sciences. Nobody knew whether I had failed cookery or simply neglected to take the exam and an investigation petered out because nobody was interested. I had spent the year before these exams perfecting my table tennis on tables put up in the girls' shed. By then 'Bert' Lau had been joined by other east Asians and they had brought to the school a new dimension: we suddenly became rather good at badminton and table tennis. Actually, very good. I put a good deal of effort into my game – bat held in the way they taught us, between first and second fingers, with the thumb cupping the back of the handle – none into the exams. Nobody did: we were way too cool. We were so isolated from the world, so full of ourselves and so unthinking that we never really wondered where all of this would lead.

Thankfully, in that interview with Mr Leimdorfer, there was another teacher present. The deputy head, tiny Mrs Plant, neatly dressed in a pink trouser suit, who never raised her voice or changed her facial expression through an entire course of Cambridge Latin, astonished me by smiling. Quite broadly. 'I think Justin will change,' she said.

I did.

People (all right, my wife, who trained as a biochemist) laugh when I say I took an A-Level in sociology. A joke subject. A kind of precursor to media studies. Tosh, poorly revealed, in too-long sentences, by faux academics who can't count or think. Well, OK. At its fringes, the subject is difficult to defend. But for me, the rescue, the change, the academic awakening, came as much from sociology as from my other A-Level subjects, English and history; from the use of irony in *Mansfield Park* or the parliamentary duels of Disraeli and Gladstone. How infinitely more fascinating was the sociological revelation that science – that smelly set of subjects that had entirely passed me by – was so hugely affected by socially constructed paradigms. Thank you, Thomas Kuhn, for this insight, contained in *The Structure of Scientific Revolutions*, which was written in the year I was born and communicated to me when I was exactly ready to hear it in 1978.

We didn't go as far as reading the book, of course, but we had the concept presented to us in bite-size chunks and we heard his name, alluring, glamorously foreign, with an 'h' in that apparently random place. I was an instant fan, a Kuhnite. It made me (along with a generation of humanities-focused softies) feel superior to those nitwits in goggles and white coats because we knew, even as they mixed their potions in blissful ignorance of their paradigm-created motives, why they were actually doing it. They thought they were gradually extending human knowledge. What I learned from Kuhn was that they were powered as well by the turmoil and angst of human intellectual competition and the attractiveness or otherwise of ideas that challenge a status quo.

What an interesting idea, too, that elites govern all societies, not just autocracies. The idea of 'circulation of elites', popularized by a chap called Vilfredo Pareto writing in prewar Italy, seemed hugely relevant in a boarding school. You can change government; hell, you can have an actual revolution supported by the masses, but in the end what you get is the top people from each tradition or strand of opinion winning out and grudgingly respecting each other. They are, always, the bosses. The chumps who back them, thinking they are going to get change, very rarely do. Or they get it but find they are in no more control than they were before because all they have done is replace one elite with another. It was electrifyingly fascinating. I think Pareto may have fallen out of fashion in sociology owing to it having been noticed that his ideas had been taken up with vigour by prewar Italian fascists, but this little-remembered Italian geezer was a good friend to me.

And what is Marxism, exactly? This last question was hugely thrilling to long-haired pseudo-revolutionaries and I developed a fine appreciation of Surplus Value, Marx's insight that, when you work for a business, you get a little less back in wages than the worth of what you put in, with the 'surplus' nicked by the running-dog capitalist. So, much more than declining '*avoir*', or buggering about with isosceles triangles, or any of the other schoolwork I had ever, reluctantly and poorly, done before, this felt properly engaging and properly useful information. How could society carry on in the knowledge of this stuff? Wasn't everyone aware of it?

Foolish, lacking in rigour, lacking in moral courage, lacking everywhere in everything, we stumbled on. And, amid the bleakness, we found, gradually, that we were stumbling towards something. At Sidcot, and around the nation, one of those famous winds of change was in the air. We were beginning to progress. In its final years, the decade was finding its feet. We grew up; it grew up. Did we begin to notice the horrors, the bullying, the misery around us as the country did in the run-up to 1979? Did we rebel as we should have?

Perhaps.

The school motto was Sic Vos Non Vobis. Roughly translated, For You But Not Yours. We were being handed something precious which we, in turn, were expected to hand on to future generations. Batons were being passed. A chain of good deeds stretching backwards and forwards, linking us all, through times of trouble, wars and hardship, to times of plenty. Not ours to keep. Not ours to break.

Like Deep Purple on tour, we trashed them in those early years. We broke those batons into a thousand pieces. We could not have cared less. Only towards the end, as the eighties approached and adulthood beckoned, did we stop to think of the state of our legacy.

First, though, the school had to come to terms with the pickle it was in.

One of the oddities of Sidcot was that it had previously been gentler and the teaching genuinely adventurous and progressive. The art teacher, Jim Bradley, was, in my day, a wizened and sad figure who would peer over your shoulder and sigh as you tried and failed to render a Coca-Cola can in pencil on sugar paper. But Bradley in his earlier years had been a fan of Bauhaus and a believer in the power of education to stimulate, to create, particularly in the breaking down of barriers between arts and crafts. He had been a serious man, one of those people who gets called 'an educationalist'. He taught at Sidcot for thirty years and I suspect there will be those with more talent than I who look back on his influence with affection. By the time I left the school he was exhausted and frustrated.

Like Britain, Sidcot had become hidebound, sclerotic, putrid. The teaching methods that had energized classrooms in the late 1960s, in Mr Bradley's heyday, getting children interested, abandoning learning by rote, joining things together rather than teaching in silos – all of this had been adopted by Sidcot. But they couldn't bring it off. Teaching lost its discipline and gained nothing much in return. It was not old-school, it was not new-school. It was a dazed mishmash. Nobody knew what they were trying to achieve, least of all us, the pupils. Were we interested in exams? We didn't know. Should we just learn for the sake of it? Well, perhaps, but how? And what if we couldn't be bothered?

Sidcot had removed academic stress but largely kept to the old-school approach to rules and regulations. Like the nation. The 1970s were full of rules that no longer protected; rules that now caused harm and whose reasons for being no one could fully remember. Closed shops. Executive toilets (or lavatories, as I would have said). Ways of doing things. Rules about manning and who could do what. It was as if we were all frightened of what the future held: half-knew, perhaps, that change was around the corner but couldn't quite face it. The whole of Britain operated in the manner that royal protocol still does: lots of nonsensical directives involving titles and forelock-tugging that are presented as olde-worlde wisdom but were actually made up last Tuesday.

Well, we had a good deal of similar edicts at Sidcot, many of them pertaining, even when we were seventeen or eighteen years old, to bedtime. A student teacher called Nicholas Kinloch arrived at Sidcot when I was in the sixth form. He was young and enthusiastic and black. We were unfamiliar with any of these characteristics but those of us who had been on the Anti-Nazi League march were determined to make him our own. Mr Kinloch taught the French Revolution. His lessons differed from what we were used to because he encouraged discussion in the manner of a university seminar. It was gloriously grown-up. And – even more of a difference – outside lessons, instead of only discussing hair length or sport, Mr Kinloch wanted to talk more about revolution, about life in France in 1789, about guillotines and purges. And he suggested doing it over a late-evening beer.

We were caught. Three sixth-formers, seventeen years old, having a beer with Mr Kinloch in his room, discussing Robespierre. We had to go and see the new headmaster. Who, in spite of himself, felt he had to give us a dressing-down for breaking the rules and came close to sending Mr Kinloch back to Liverpool University to begin his post-graduate teaching qualification all over again, owing to an inability to get to grips with Quaker education. Luckily, this did not happen. But our teacher looked chastened, reduced, and we traipsed back into class that day aware that something had changed: it had become fully obvious to all of us that this place was ludicrous. We were spending half our time in the Amnesty International group campaigning against arbitrary punishment and the rest imposing, or having imposed on us, the meaningless rigours of an incompetently run prison camp.

It had to stop. The new headmaster helped. He could see the future even if he couldn't get there. And he was not alone. A remarkable teacher called Martin Bell sought me out one day in the playground, shortly after my A-Level interview with the head and his deputy – the day I resolved to do better, to think of the future beyond the Mendip Hills. We liked Mr Bell. He was a cod disciplinarian, given to mock outbursts of temper and long stares of disapproval that would end in a vulpine grin. He seemed as troubled as we were. He wasn't much older than thirty or so, tweedily dressed, breath smelling, eyes bloodshot, skin mottled, hair unwashed and greasy. 'Let's get on,' he would mutter to himself, for no obvious reason, as he marched round the school, books held across his chest under his right arm, the other swinging in an exaggerated arc like a broken clockwork toy soldier.

'Ah, Webb.'

'Sir.'

'There is a qualification in British Constitution, halfway between O- and A-Level, and you shall do it and I shall teach it and we begin tomorrow.'

Good old Mr Bell. What on earth was he doing, what on earth was anyone doing, teaching at Sidcot then? One or two, like poor Mr Bradley, had just got stuck. They lived in the village and saw the seasons come and go and the children's hair get longer, then shorter, and alarms and excursions jangle and pass. But mostly they were misfits for whom things had gone badly wrong. They lived in putrid little flats around the school. A history teacher with a fob watch told us he admired the feudal system because everyone knew where they were. The tragedy was that it was his first job out of university. He had huge glasses and never smiled. Children know things, even in the 1970s. We steered clear of him.

Others, like my English teacher, Grace Holden, we came to adore. 'One day,' she told us, 'we might all live as they do in *The Machine Stops*.' Bloody hell, she was right. Visionary. As visionary as E. M. Forster, whose short story of that name is a dystopian science-fiction piece about a society where all contact is through a machine and everyone is connected only by screens. There were flashes of genuine learning at Sidcot.

And Mr Bell was determined to add to them. He seemed to be playing a part, the role of a public-school master at a decent school, an Uppingham or a Harrow where there was a proper school song, a recognizable tie, an old boys' network that could one day get you into Boodle's. Whatever his motivation, he saw me as a mission.

We sat, every week for a year, in his foul-smelling study, and he lectured me straight from the syllabus. Bagehot. The Fulton Report of 1968. The Cabinet. He spoke, I wrote. The power of the prime minister. Committees of the Whole House. It could not have been drier – the whole subject stank of stale whisky. And Mr Bell offered not one moment of reflection or discussion, not one single nod in the direction of modernity.

It suited me perfectly. I was captivated. Something clicked. At the end of the summer term, I took an exam and, for the first time in my life, passed with flying colours. Nothing had ever stuck before. But ask me today about Lord Hailsham on elective dictatorship or the Heath government's invention of the Central Policy Review Staff and I can still bore you to death with the pros and cons of early 1970s fears about extremism in the Commons or efforts to co-ordinate strategy across government departments. This was British Constitution as an intellectual firestorm: uncodified, unbound. A rescue mission.

Thus British Constitution, alongside sociology, was my salvation. I owe this man a huge debt. I am no Albert Camus. My circumstances were not as poor as those of the great French writer, nor my successes as great (to put it mildly), but Camus' famous letter to his former teacher when he received the Nobel Prize for Literature always puts me in mind of Mr Bell. 'Without you,' he wrote, 'without the affectionate hand you extended to the small poor child that I was, without your teaching and example, none of all this would have happened.'

While I was in the midst of this period of academic awakening – this ultra-mini enlightenment – Mr Leimdorfer personally toured the school in a way the other head, the other teachers, never had. And discovered, at first hand, its idiosyncrasies. Is that the right word? Perhaps not. A friend in the sixth form had stolen a motorbike. The police had come to the school. Mr Leimdorfer went to my friend's study and found him face down with a vodka bottle next to him. The officers were told it was an inconvenient moment and asked if they could come back later, which, as we were Quakers, they agreed to do.

But the vodka was low-level depravity by our standards.

In 1978, in the changing rooms on a Saturday evening after a rugby match, I watched a boy inject something into a vein. He was no longer at the school – he was the older brother of someone in my year – but, like many former pupils in those days, he would come back to loll about, to buy and sell booze or dope, maybe to get a girl, steal a radio, chat to a teacher, hang loose.

Or, on this occasion, to shoot up. He had arrived in the school on a motorbike which he revved insolently in the playground. He was wearing loons, those ludicrous trousers that flared from the thigh, and a loose muslin top. It was two years since Paul Kossoff, the guitarist of Free, had died of the effects of drug abuse during a night flight from Los Angeles to New York. Kossoff's death was a sickly-sweet event at our school. It was shocking but, frankly, it added to his glamour in our eyes. In Quakerly fashion, we sympathized with Kossoff's father, David, a well-known actor who became an anti-drugs campaigner of some note. But we were in love with our idea of Paul for all he was, including, horribly, that he was dead.

So I was fascinated, and tried not to be repelled, as this boy flicked at his inner arm in the changing rooms that day, finding a vein, sealing it off, taking out the syringe. It says something of the social mores of the school that I was more shocked by something he said than by what he was doing. 'I'm having such little luck with the chicks these days, I'm thinking of moving on to men.'

My first thought was: wow, steady on. You could shoot up in Sidcot in 1978 without fear of social ostracism but this same-sex talk was still highly dangerous territory. I muttered something about wishing him better luck with the chicks. A bell went somewhere, signifying tea. Languidly rung, by a boy who couldn't care less. In a school that had lost the ability to care at all.

Perhaps it was time for us to reassess. Perhaps our generation, without quite knowing why, began the fightback against the depravity: the drugs, the bullying, the uselessness of it all.

At that very moment, in the swirling seas of the age, anchorless, rudderless, taking on water, the ship began to right itself, to find direction; the storm miraculously to abate. The national ship was still some way off the certainty and purpose of the Thatcher years but at Sidcot, my year group, brought together in adversity, found its own purpose and, in a limited way, redemption. We changed the weather, at least a little.

Self-awareness helped.

What those of us who played competitive sport began to notice, in our last years at Sidcot, was that we were odd. We underperformed in sport in part because we were a small gene pool. Up the road at Chew Valley Comprehensive they had a thousand kids. But it was more than that. When we played Chew we seemed so gauche, so weird, so

unworldly. We had become trapped, infantilized, aware
with growing horror of the Quaker fakery that told us we
were especially nice when in fact we were especially . . .
nothing much.

Even Mr Sisman, the games master with the temper, was
a more relaxed presence. I think he stopped beating the
younger children. He tried hard to teach me to swim.
Amnesty International still made no sense to him: 'Horses
for courses' was his comment on whether people should
be sprung from jail in foreign countries – meaning, I suppose, that they needed to take heed of the powers that be
when thinking their thoughts. But he said it with a sigh.
The malice that had infected us all in the early part of the
decade, and infected pupils as much as teachers, seemed,
as 1980 approached, to have dissipated if not disappeared.
My memory of Mr Sisman, in the end, is of a genial person.
For all the faults of the school, none of the teachers was a
psychopath. It says something about the 1970s that this
marks the place out as vaguely special, but it does. Perhaps
the Quakers can be a little bit proud of that. Mind you, I
don't include pupils in that blanket exculpation. Several of
them displayed psychopathic traits, and continued to do
so to the end, possibly into later life.

And the rest of us? Jonathan Aitken, the disgraced,
imprisoned and now rehabilitated former MP, boasted that
prison would be no problem for him after boarding school
and he was right: not because of the hardships but because
of the camaraderie and the ability developed by anyone

who goes to boarding school to find their place, their level, their role in the organism. To be bullied, to bully. To pass from one condition to the next. To live this experience.

It changed me. I wonder, as I get older, whether our boarding-school brains are wired differently from most other people's. Neuroscience research suggests that variations in what psychologists call 'cultural self-construal' can result in differences in brain activation. As Bruce Hood puts it in his enthralling book *Possessed*: 'Brain activation differs between individuals from independent and collectivist cultures when it comes to a number of tasks.'

Perhaps this is why I don't care when other family members take my stuff. Hood's book doesn't mention school life but Sidcot was the epitome of collectivism. We *were* all in it together. We owned nothing. Hood would say that our brains were more attuned to the collective. This certainly allows for vertical growth – boarding schools are full of tall poppies – but their success is geared to the horizontal, to the functioning of the whole community. The sense of community is not just foisted on you by lustily singing the school song. It's actually in your head, in your brain.

This is a good thing, on balance. It allowed me to understand intuitively that society does, actually, exist. And, however accomplished any of us become, nothing of me is outside the whole. This helped me. Was it privilege? Perhaps.

∾

On my last day at school I was overcome with melancholy. I was eighteen, waiting for the car – driven for the last time by little Den Davis – to come and take me home. My trunk was packed. All my possessions were ready to move. And yet, of course, I had no home. This was home. Prisoners must feel the same after the end of a long sentence. Yes, it will be nice to walk about in the sunshine. But what will life be like without the clanking of the doors, the rattle of the keys? I was sitting in a room in the main part of the school that smelled of sweetly rotting wood. Most of my erstwhile friends had already left.

Around me, as I sat in maudlin solitude, were bookcases that had been there for a century or more. Histories of the school, bound volumes full of hearty stories of discovery and growth. I took one out and stole it: a bit of the school that I would keep. Who possessed whom? In the Robert Frost poem 'The Gift Outright' (which I didn't know then), he explains American post-revolution patriotism by pointing out that it was a two-way process:

> But we were England's, still colonials,
> Possessing what we still were unpossessed by,
> Possessed by what we now no more possessed.
> Something we were withholding made us weak
> Until we found out that it was ourselves
> We were withholding from our land of living,
> And forthwith found salvation in surrender.

Plenty of Sidcot children eventually found salvation in surrender. I did not. After I had left, I found my relationship with the place strange. It tugged in an unsatisfactory way. Had the school made me? Would it be good to pretend it had anyway? And what does all this intensity do to anyone's ability to navigate their way through life? To build one-to-one relationships, romantic, professional, just ordinarily social, when all you have known is the crowd, the clan, is bewildering. Or it would be to me. Of course, you have one-to-one relationships at school, with teachers like dear Mr Bell, with girls you 'were going out with', even though there was no 'out' to go to. But the web of the tribe, the context of closeness, the oddness, in school, of anyone who developed anything more exclusive; this has an impact, I reckon, that can last a lifetime. If you're lucky, you have a group at university, even at work. You have a family in later life. But none of these match the experience of growing up in a pack. Particularly in a feral pack like ours.

I wanted, when I left, to truly feel the whole 'best days of your life' package of immediate, genuine, foolish nostalgia. It wouldn't come. In a moment of keenness or desperation, in my first year in the school I had attempted to be a Christian. I had spent an entire hour's Sunday Meeting imagining there was a God and that he was speaking to me. I tried everything. I so contorted my silent self that the girl sitting next to me, jolly, smiley Tessa, who, in other circumstances, I would have been thrilled to find taking an interest in my well-being, whispered, 'Are you OK?' I had found no easy way to explain my quest. And for me, that was it, as far as religion was concerned, for a lifetime.

I tried similarly, and failed similarly, with the old school sentimentality thing. Once again defeated, I gave up.

Had I grown? What had I discovered? Sidcot was badly run and criminally lax but we didn't really help much. Yes, we were young. But the young step up to plates in all manner of situations. Fourteen-year-old Tom Leimdorfer had witnessed the tanks rolling into Budapest. In more recent times, Malala Yousafzai stood up to the Taliban. I know, I know. We are not all cut from the cloth of the brave. But we were, we are, a pretty pampered generation. Sidcot's pupils had once been made of sterner stuff. On that last day, as I leafed through the old scholars' books, I ached to do it all again, only this time properly. Read the damned books. Listen. Too late.

I had retaken O-Level maths. It was a struggle, not for me, but for the poor man, a new teacher, who was tasked with getting a group of us through the exam. The first attempt was a disaster: we all went down a grade. This was a source of enormous hilarity. But by this time the new vibe I have mentioned was beginning to take effect. Half of me, perhaps more than half of me, was half-wondering if this insouciant stance was a sensible plan. Perhaps failure, if it really was going to end in a doss house in Somerset, smoking weed and listening to Barclay James Harvest, was not all that we had convinced ourselves it was cracked up to be. The school too, under the new head, had come round to a view of education in which maths might be seen as quite important.

They came together, my late-found seriousness of purpose and the school's reluctant emergence from its world of indolent cruelty, and a glorious thing emerged: a C-grade pass in maths at the third attempt.

From wastrel to professor. Never has the journey been so meteoric. I took three A-Levels – English, history and sociology – and got three B grades, a huge deal in a school from which most children did not go to university. I knew something had changed for me. I tore up my plans for a degree from a minor-league university and took a year off to re-apply for just one: the London School of Economics, where the serious people were.

I would never play table tennis again.

7

Boys Will Be Boys

In the mid-1970s, without it being a conscious thing, of course, I began to search for men, or manhood, by watching rugby. Rugby Union at all levels was a dire game in those days, fantastically vicious, drunken and wild at its fringes, a home for thugs and – as the West Country locals called them – 'mentalists'. For me, fatherless, manless, cognizant of no masculinity outside school other than the type constructed by Mum, or the damaged kind represented by Charles, it was fabulously seductive. Lightheaded, slightly giddy, I would pay my 50p to the men at the gate to watch Bath play: there was no turnstile, no advance booking. You just wandered in.

None of the stories Mum told of the men in her life filled me with confidence in my sex. Her own father was a man she seemed genuinely in awe of but also a wretched specimen. Leonard Crocombe was an editor of magazines and a writer of books of jokes and little stories designed to bring smiles to faces but nothing much else. He was also a friend of Lord Reith and the first editor of the *Radio Times*. His posh wife (dear Granny, who we had wrapped, ineptly, in newspaper) had been, perhaps, a useful prop but little more to him than that. After the war he left her in a way that postwar men still could: in penury.

I met him only once, ushered into a room where I suppose he was dying, but I knew his legacy well. My dear little granny's poverty was a direct result of the way women could be deserted in those days. Leonard went to live in the National Liberal Club and, my mother said, spent all his money on his room and board.

She was mildly annoyed about that, but never quite enough, it seemed to me. Leonard was driven and successful; that much I understood. Much more of a man in that respect than Charles. More in the mould of my father, whose name we didn't mention. Not much of a role model, though. Not much of a man. I hate the phrase 'role model' – it's plodding and unrealistic, as if anyone actually identifies another individual and decides to emulate them. But we grow up with pointers, do we not? Examples of this and that approach to life working, and not working, and, as we grow older, we can sort out what we think. It is no bad thing if some of the good ones, or at least one of them, is a man.

At school I played rugby with increasing vigour and ability and during the winter holidays I would take myself to the Recreation Ground in the centre of Bath to see the mentalists at play. On a cold Saturday afternoon this was, and still is, a place of wonderment, of maleness. Floodlights had recently been bought. The smell of hot dogs – unhealthy food (*working-class* food) – wafted from a single stand. In those days, Rugby Union was an amateur game and although Bath were one of the best sides in the country their team was a group of local men – solicitors, builders, farmers – who liked violence and beer. They practised a bit on Tuesdays but there was little more to it than that.

The crowd on a Saturday afternoon was not exactly a crowd, more a kind of apologetic weekly hook-up of a few hundred large, often misshapen, men and their assorted equally misshapen wives and girlfriends. It was a cauldron of West Countrydom: 'All right, my luvver?' was the greeting of choice. The stock reply: 'Mustn't grumble'. Cigars were smoked. There was a stand on one side of the ground but the other was completely open. You just stood there behind the linesman. A single loudspeaker blared martial music until a few minutes before battle, when the teams would be read out. This was the extent of the pre-match build-up.

It was shambolic and uncomfortable. When it rained you got wet. On windy days it was piercingly cold. People hugged themselves on the touchline. Often on the pitch, too: wingers in those days seldom got much to do and had none of the benefits of modern kit. In ill-fitting shorts and baggy cotton tops they stood frozen to the spot or hopped from foot to foot waiting for some action. The pitch itself was a disgrace by modern standards. You couldn't have put animals on it: boggy, rutted, with patches of grass and sand to soak up the water.

But it was glorious, too. I drank it in. The cheers when the teams jogged out. The stamping at scrum time. The opposing packs crying 'Heavy!' as they clattered into each other. The embarrassing masculine pointlessness of it all. The mud. The blood: it was everywhere in those pre-AIDS days and nobody cared. Even at school we bled throughout matches. At Bath it stained shirts, heads, arms and legs. 'Let's do the business!' was the battle cry of one of the most aggressive players of that generation. He meant 'Let's destroy our opponents' manhood,' and he often did, squeezing, gouging, brutalizing. I lapped it up. Occasionally, experimentally, I yelped encouragement, but mostly I kept silent: a witness to all this havoc, a ghost passing along the touchline (there were so few people there that you could trot around the field following the action more or less as you pleased), noticing everything, properly involved in none of it.

Once, when we were playing Llanelli, a winger called John Davies, a wiry little guy, was standing right in front of me as one of the giants of the game, the Llanelli and Wales fly-half Phil Bennett, came swerving towards him. Bennett, to this day one of rugby's greatest men, was a magician, a side-stepper, a twinkletoes. But he was also rock-hard, physically toughened by long experience of what transpired when the side-step failed and a group of marauding forwards pummelled his guts out. So he was no mean sight coming down the wing. I would have let him pass.

Everything in my upbringing would have told me to let him pass. He was famous and revered and male to his toes. Possibly angry. And, my mother would have pointed out, sweaty, too – unclean and uncouth. If he was so keen to get that piece of leather to the other end of the pitch, why not let him? It really should not be a matter of life and death.

Davies, the Bath player, had other ideas. He hurled himself at the celebrated man, catching him painfully on the lower thighs and thumping him over the muddy touchline. They both landed no more than a yard from my feet. And, as they rose, Davies said, with quiet venom, 'You don't like being tackled, do you, you flash fucker.'

And with that, they carried on. One man had tried to get to the tryline. The other had stopped him and snarled. The referee called for a lineout. The players assembled and prepared for the next stage of battle. Davies had brought Bennett down and, far from apologizing, far from feeling awkward, had danced on the metaphorical grave of his opponent. He had rubbed it in. And yet – how could this be? – the two men were later to shake hands and grin the sheepish grins of chaps who have fought and then stopped fighting.

Rugby is a game of physical intimidation. For many boys, the physicality is a bit of fun but stays with them no longer than the game itself. For me it was a source of ever-increasing and deep-seated self-doubt. When I was taking part, I found it difficult to laugh off being hit. It upset me much more than it should have done. Like a moth to a flame, I was drawn to watching Bath play. The added levels of violence and forgiveness for violence fascinated me. At the end of the game the players would drape arms round each other. The crowd would be on the pitch with them for a final melee of mingling in the mud; the combatants, gaping flesh wounds badly bandaged, would hoist kids on to their shoulders, chat to their mums and dads, and share war stories with the chaps from the other team. You could get close enough to smell the wintergreen.

As the steam rose into the darkening sky from the flanks of these gnarled giants, I could imagine myself one of them, comfortable enough in my own skin, in my male body, to have thumped and been thumped and now to be laughing about it. To have spat out a tooth on the halfway line and not given a damn. To be scarred and all the more attractive for the scarring. All the more confident. This was what I wanted more than anything on those evenings, as I trudged home. Camaraderie, bravery, a joint endeavour that broke the loneliness, above all in a masculine incarnation. But I knew in my heart I had been feminized. I was sensitive to a fault; aware of too much.

'Was it good, dear?' Mum would ask, looking up from the *Guardian* as I got home.

Yes, it was good. But I was not part of it.

Jean-Paul Sartre was no rugby player and I was no reader in those days (apart from Jennings), but the existentialist philosopher would have been known to my mother, who was by now well into the serious and thoughtful period of her life, and certainly acquainted with the work of his partner, Simone de Beauvoir. I have already suggested that de Beauvoir's views on 'otherness' were deeply relevant in our home. Her view of femininity conjured up for me, when I read it in later life, my own early experience. Mum would have understood that her son lived as Sartre and de Beauvoir said all women lived. Sartre puts it like this. Suppose you are looking through a keyhole. You are in a hotel corridor but you are alone. You are concentrating on what is happening on the other side of the door. It doesn't matter what it is: the point is that you are looking at it. It is the object of your attention. Then someone, a maid perhaps, comes along the corridor. She looks at you. You are now both the subject, the looker, and the object: the looked at. You have changed. Even if you are not embarrassed about what you are doing, the situation is altered by the addition of the other person. You are now what Sartre calls a 'self for others', a self whose full meaning and existence can only be captured by them, not by you.

The contention is that this is part of why women are perceived as 'the second sex', living always as if being watched, living always with the sense that they do not own themselves. This is what feminization can do: it plays with the ability of a boy to be fully a boy. And, of course, it plays equally with the ability of a girl to be a girl. In many respects, being brought up with more femininity than masculinity can be a good thing. Unembarrassed kindness, no fear of physical affection, and above all empathy – a glorious ability to see others' travails as your own – can be yours.

But being a 'self for others' is a strain. A strain for all unliberated womanhood. A strain for the child I was. On the rugby field, even in the crowd, you cannot relax. Your inadequacy is laid bare.

In the modern world we think (rightly) that boys are improved by the influence of strong women. A mother who works. An elder sister who has travelled the world. Mum was certainly strong in the sense of surviving. She knew her mind. But a boy brought up by a woman effectively alone can be a boy reduced in the scope of his being. An example: I could not swim. Mum thought this was fine. Of course, there are other single mums for whom this might be more of a concern but generally, the feminine way is to take growing up seriously and slowly. Swimming was for another day. Mum had zero interest in sport. A father – my concept of a traditional father, a good father – might have pointed out that being the only child in a class of thirty who had to sit by the pool was not a place you wanted to be in. Might have seen the value of trying even if it made you splutter. Might have said, 'Let's learn together.' Not swimming festered. It became 'being afraid of water'. It followed me down the years. It need not have.

A good father might have done a better job of buying a jockstrap, too. It was the seriousness with which this purchase was considered that has lived in my memory down the ages. Jockstraps were a thing before men just gave up, got normal and wore pants for sport. In the 1970s you had to buy a place to put your balls. You had to go upstairs in a musty sports shop in the centre of Bath and sit in a room the size of a garden shed while the issue of size was considered. Should it be small? Very small? Oh God, please, just buy the damned thing. It was for weekly school football and it was probably compulsory but what a fuss. Men's stuff as seen through the eyes of this woman, as handed down to her son.

There was no carelessness in our home. We laughed but we seldom giggled. I shrink from male and female stereotypes; yes, of course there are careless women and uptight men, but I have seen enough of proper family life, including my own when my children were young, to know that men can be a different sort of parent and that it matters.

Of course, it was more than this. I was a substitute in Mum's life for the companionship she couldn't find elsewhere. That companionship – with a man or a woman – would have reduced the intensity of us. It might have allowed for carelessness to creep in. I remember telling a friend once that my mother had sacrificed everything for me and the friend replying with a glance that said, 'That's not quite the story, is it?' It is not.

There are many children who look after adults, usually disabled or sick single parents. Often heroically. I was no hero but I was, in another sense, a carer. I was an emotional support. Actually, more: I was a lover. We play the roles we are given. Submission is not a sin. I told Mum once that my perfect holiday would be the two of us together, staying in bed. I remember the moment: it was a crisp, autumn day and we were standing around a bonfire in the garden, burning leaves. She half laughed off the oddness of it. I think I recall a frisson of withdrawal, perhaps a start, a temporary quickening of the atmosphere, but no more than that.

I wonder, though: did that remark give her pause? We were an item in my early days, for better or worse, for richer or poorer. But did she determine then that the time had come to throw the only thing in the world she loved on to the back of the lorry that would take him to a place where he would have a happier childhood? Was this the day when the decision to send me to boarding school was taken? I cannot remember whether this was before or after the incident with the deprived child who never came. That certainly seemed at the time to be relevant. She hinted in later life that boarding school had only happened because of Charles; that the need to get away from him had trumped all else. But was it due as much to a fear of the relationship she had created? Was that what went through her mind that afternoon by the bonfire? The leaves were damp and the fire hugely smoky. The evidence of our work curled up and up until the wind blew it back at us and sent us, eyes stinging, inside.

~

To all of this the single mothers (or those who are effectively single) of only sons might justifiably retort: well, thanks for the retrospective assessment, but what was the alternative? Intensity and oddness is a by-product of the thing that is useful in this relationship; more than useful. The superpower it has: love.

In a larger family the feeling can, of course, be as intense, but the mechanics might be looser. Plenty of families that function more normally are just as loving. But in a family of a couple, there is the couple. With more than one child, there are the other children. With a dog, there is a dog. With us, there was me. And that was it. Mum had no other focus and I had no other lodestar.

The effect of this is to supercharge the part of any person that gives them not just confidence but resilience, too. For all my eccentricity and my fear about my eccentricity, I knew as well that I was brilliantly gifted because she told me I was. Actually, she did more than that: she acted as if I was without saying so. And by the time it became obvious that I was not brilliantly gifted, it no longer mattered. There is some internal switch that is flicked by the love of a parent at this level of brightness and constancy. Once it has been flicked, it stays on.

Those sociologists I admired at school knew this well. The upper social classes, they pointed out, had the ability to inculcate in their children a view of authority that protected them from harm. They owned it. Even when things went wrong they had no fear of social failure because they called the shots. It's more subtle, way more, than being 'posh' or 'rich'. It is being entitled, but in a perfectly reasonable, comfortable way; feeling OK about taking what is yours. About having what you deserve, and maybe a bit extra. Nowadays it might be called 'white privilege'. You don't have to be a hereditary peer to possess it. It can live in the heads, in the hearts, of much less august personages. Including, at 90 Wells Road, me.

So, in spite of the fact that my stepfather collected garage doors and attempted suicide, that my real father read the news in another world, that visiting Mrs Lock was the best fun I could have, that my mother had such a peculiar, class-damaged view of mankind; in spite of all these things, I knew from an early age that I belonged. Here, in England, I had a place. To their enormous credit, most of those who knew my mother seemed to indulge her exalted view of me: I was never aware of any blowback. I think they mostly pitied our circumstances and were unaware of just how much the weight of her affection could make up for all else. If there was privilege in my upbringing, this was it. In spite of all the oddness, the occasional horror, the shambolic aimlessness of so much of my early life, I can still feel her arms around me.

In truth she played close to the edge, did Mum. She decided either that academic success was beneath me or that I wouldn't achieve it. Hence the lack of interest in my O-Levels, the failure to see a potential problem when I gave up all the sciences so early. You could just about get away with this in the 1970s if you held your knife and fork properly but it was beginning (rightly, of course) to be a close-run thing. This was still the era of dim Oxbridge folk, of gentlemen's thirds in land economy or theology.

But it was all getting a bit more squeaky. Mum's assumption that the world would see I was a gentleman (and a brilliant one) was heroic but timed like a last-minute match-winning kick at Bath Rugby Club: the crowd go 'oooh!' and slap each other on the back, but the smiles they exchange whisper, 'Darn it my luvvers, close 'n' that!'

Still, even without a last-ditch play on the academic front, I might have had the self-belief and guile to get somewhere anyway. The kind of self-belief that comes entirely from being the apple of someone's eye. It is the upside of all of this, and not to be disparaged or dismissed. Without it I would surely have been even more lost than I was.

Nurture, then, was the key. And nature? The genes?

The genes, eh? We are not racehorses. Nor are we completely free, at birth, of determining or limiting factors. No, we are a mess of stuff waiting to happen, of latency and potency. The old nature-versus-nurture debate is, thankfully, played out now. Epigenetics is the way to go: the study of how some genes, or sets of genes, are nourished – switched on, in effect – by environmental factors; by what happens to us. Or doesn't. Nature *and* nurture.

My maternal grandfather was no gentleman when it came to his treatment of his wife and wider family. But he was a gentleman journalist of considerable ability. Leonard Crocombe was chosen by Lord Reith to be the first editor of the *Radio Times* because he could turn a sentence, spot a story. His joke books, utterly unmemorable and obvious to modern tastes, were successful enough back in the day. His

career could have been the model for the character Bagshaw in Anthony Powell's *A Dance to the Music of Time*:

> He possessed that opportune facility for turning out
> several thousand words on any subject whatsoever at the
> shortest possible notice: politics: sport: books: finance:
> science: art: fashion – as he himself said, 'War, Famine,
> Pestilence or Death on a Pale Horse'. All were equal
> when it came to Bagshaw's typewriter.

I wonder if Powell, a young novelist and posh London
partygoer at the time of the *Radio Times'* establishment,
might have met my grandfather. Like Bagshaw, Leonard
Crocombe could write cogently and fast. Nothing flashy.
Nothing outlasting his death. Nothing that will trouble
future generations. I sensed from an early age that I had
inherited that. I am not saying I did inherit it, merely that
I sensed it, and that, I am going to argue, is important.

And, of course, there may be inheritance on two sides.
My actual father was unquestionably among the more able
reporters of his hugely talented, if booze-damaged, generation. Like my grandfather, Peter Woods was self-made.
And, like him, he had an ability to turn sentences, to capture attention. Peter Woods was no novelist, either, but
when you see him in online archive footage as the Berlin
Wall was going up, you recognize (I certainly do) the craft
of his journalism.

Both men had a desire to stick their noses into other
people's business and tell stories about it. And not just to

tell stories. To go further – to do what humans have done since they first sat around fires recounting to each other what had happened that day: to gather others together and hold their attention. We only understand the world through stories. Even the most desiccated scientific document must capture its readers. Both Leonard Crocombe and Peter Woods could do this.

At the end of the first academic year at prep school I was set a holiday task of keeping a diary of the summer. Like a zillion children before and since, I approached it with a sigh. But with an inheritance, too. And with help from an immediate talent, a talent unused, uncalled upon, a talent forever hidden to all but me. Yes, the two grand men of words might have left a mark, but if there were journalistic genes going, Mum was in line for some from Leonard. Throughout her life, in the dissolute times and the wise times, she had a real grasp of the power of language. She understood. Above all, she appreciated, loved, laughed over, a clever turn of phrase. So, for me, well, this was a road I wanted to travel down. Never mind the old chaps: I wanted to please Mum, and words did.

'We don't do anything,' I pointed out, about this diary project. 'Well, write about that,' she replied. Of course. Like Anthony Powell's Bagshaw, I needed to turn my hand to anything, including nothing. The diary became a dance to the music of dull days. Mordant asides about a dog ('Fido did not come in with muddy paws because he does not have muddy paws because he has not been in the

garden because he DOES NOT EXIST!'). I am not suggesting it was brilliant but, for 1969, it had a certain élan
and the school, possibly against their natural instincts,
gave it the gold prize. I suspect the other kids had written
about things that actually happened and thus displayed an
absence of journalistic genes. But Mum knew better. She
had seen journalists up close. It was the first prize for writing I ever won. And it was entirely due to my mother. To
her genes. Our genes.

Or not. Because, of course, genetic inheritance is only
part of the story and probably not a big part of it. You
inherit, too, if you are lucky, some interest in areas of life.
We had books. We had our two copies of the *Guardian*
every day in an era when the *Guardian* was broadminded
and socially liberal. During Mum's communist phase we
had the *Morning Star* as well. I think Charles took the *New
Statesman* to ward off voices in his head calling him a Tory.
Anyway, we had literature and journalism in the home. We
were acutely aware of news and the reporting of news.
That man Muggeridge on the TV. This was the world, the
whole world.

And, at exactly the right moment, Mum dropped into it
exactly the right book: the second-best book ever written
about journalism (Evelyn Waugh's *Scoop* must always and
for ever have the first prize). It left me in tears of laughter
and it still does. *The Tin Men*, Michael Frayn's first novel,
was written in 1965 but I must have first seen it in the early
1970s. It is set in a futuristic organization working to

simplify life by programming computers to perform all everyday human tasks, including producing newspapers.

A glorious lexicon of the multi-purpose monosyllables favoured by headline-writers, called Unit Headline Language, is devised, enabling the computer to knock out headlines at random. A story could be continued by adding one 'unit' to the formula each day, with 'STRIKE THREAT' followed by 'STRIKE THREAT PLEA' and 'STRIKE THREAT PLEA PROBE', and so on, culminating in 'STRIKE THREAT PLEA PROBE MOVE SHOCK HOPE STORM', or by assembling units completely at random ('RACE HATE PLEA MOVE DEAL'), resulting in 'a paper whose language was both soothingly familiar and yet calmingly incomprehensible'.

This was genius. And, to my eyes, it elevated rather than denigrated the journalistic craft. This was satire but the more it lampooned, the more I found myself loving the target of the fun: the silliness, the vacuousness of the news business. To me it gave journalism added allure, the glamour of a secret society. What Michael Frayn spotted and satirized above all was the tradecraft, the knack, and a lightness, a thoughtlessness that came alongside it. Journalism could be fun and if you could do it you could enjoy yourself.

It was also callous. And that I liked the idea of. In *Scoop* there's a moment when the country bumpkin goes up to Fleet Street to visit the offices of the newspaper for which he writes, his expectations erroneously based on a film he had once seen in Taunton 'about newspaper life in New York where neurotic men in shirt sleeves and eye-shades had rushed from telephone to tape-machines, insulting and betraying one another in circumstances of unredeemed squalor'.

This attracted me. Why? Cynicism suited my world as I grew up because, I suppose, it made sense of it. I didn't know why my father did not know me or seek to, but perhaps a celebration of the hard-bitten approach to life was a child's way of deciding this was OK. I was also living in a house where sides were being picked in battles (real and imagined) with the outside world. Charles had his view of what was happening, often deranged. Mum had hers – not deranged, but massively Manichean, by the time we reached the mid-seventies, fuelled by her hatred of nuclear weapons and her friends with their bobble hats and duffel coats. Positions had to be taken and defended. Things were black or white, good or bad. My reaction to all of this was to take solace in the cool pool of satire and to admire the characters created by Waugh and Frayn and others. In *The Tin Men*, one of them is described in a way that made me giggle admiringly: 'Haugh had an open mind. It was open at the front, and it was open at the back. Opinions, beliefs, philosophies entered, sojourned briefly, and were pushed out at the other end by the press of incoming convictions and systems.'

It is odd for children to crave a lack of certainty but I think I did. I wanted to be un-souled: I wanted to care less.

I wanted us all to be more careless, to be free of the shackles that care imposed.

So, when Michael Frayn portrayed a world of amoral, happy-go-lucky, word-clever, here-today-gone-tomorrow shysters, well, what was not to like? When Evelyn Waugh's scalpel cut to the deepest quick of the silliness of journalism, bring it on. These were my people. Plenty of journalists go into the trade in order to do good. It can be an act of public service. Lifting the lid, shining the light, speaking truth to power. I wanted not much more than Michael Frayn's Unit Headline Language machine and an expense account. And, working alongside the serious and intense colleagues I have had down the years, I have spotted plenty of fellow seekers after fun. Perhaps they, too, would seek to expiate their crimes against seriousness by pointing out that they had their fill of seriousness early in life. Maybe we are a type.

I suppose I could have followed another path. But once it became obvious that coach-driving was not going to please Mum, there was, in truth, little else for me to do. I was never going to be a scientist or a mathematician, and not (just) because I didn't possess the ability. Dear Mum could barely count and saw no use in trying. Forget about the genes, or lack of them, what matters here is the voice that says 'Well done' when you write a clever sentence and offers only a vague 'Never mind, dear' when you struggle with an equation.

But what about the 'talent' that can turn an event into

something someone might read about – that talent Leonard Crocombe and Peter Woods and Mum all had, to a greater or lesser degree? I take the Matthew Syed view. In making his arguments about the nature of success, the journalist and former English table-tennis champion cites the example of the talent shown by him and his brother for table tennis. In fact, the street where he grew up in Reading produced an extraordinary number of English table-tennis stars of both sexes in the early 1980s. This was not something in the water and it was unlikely to be pure coincidence, either. It was practice. A good coach, a local club. An enthusiasm that seized a group of children. It led Syed to write a now-famous book analysing success in which he contends that 'talent' doesn't exist in the absence of opportunity and, if opportunity is stressed, then talent is, miraculously, found.

True. I may have inherited the minor-league ability to write minor-league stuff but far more important have been the encouragement and the opportunities to do it. It is not particularly strange that I do (roughly) the same job as my father did or grandfather. It would be stranger if I didn't. Teachers who are the sons and daughters of teachers will know this. Doctors, too. Maybe even coach drivers. In Henry Moore's memoirs, he describes rubbing his mother's rheumatic back with oil. Aha, you think, as you look at his statues – all those huge, smooth, female forms. Oh, he had talent, but the talent, the sculpture, was itself shaped by circumstance, experience, life.

That's the writing side of it. But what makes a child a show-off, to use the old-fashioned term that would certainly have been used of me? In particular, what makes an insular, shy, self-effacing, socially unconfident, overweight, unhappy child want to take to the stage, any stage, any time, with any material? Why did Narcissus fall in love with his own image?

I remember my fall. It was long before the Dymond Speech competition and long before a loud rendition of Shakespeare's Sir Toby Belch in a school production of *Twelfth Night*. Yes, I gave 'a plague o' these pickle-herring!' a bit of welly that lesser Sidcot thespians (which was most of them) might not have managed, but this was not the pool into which Narcissus gazed. That was encountered even before the *Woman's Hour* letter about rape.

Much earlier, in fact, and the audience was as peculiar as the performer. We had bought a cassette-recorder. It had been a Significant Purchase and, as such, the acquisition of this new and perhaps flighty area of entertainment had taken us a year or so to mull over (it did indeed turn out to be short-lived, if not quite as speedily overtaken as Mum feared). But when it finally came it allowed me, for the first time, to hear my voice on tape.

It was awful. I sounded like Roy Plomley. No disrespect to the creator and long-time presenter of *Desert Island Discs* but, even in the 1970s, Roy's cut-glass accent felt a touch . . . dated. Mum sounded like the Queen. The two of us marvelled at this technology like cave-people given a kaleidoscope. Mum lost interest; I did not. And this is where the performance began. The comparison with Roy Plomley was made by a friend of Mum's to whom she had mentioned the cassette-recorder. The friend – Betty was her name – was a grande dame of Bath society and wished, she said, that she might one day be on *Desert Island Discs*. We had a deal.

I think I was eight. Betty was dotty. She had done not one interesting thing in her whole naval-officer-wedded life. She had children but expressed no interest in them. It taught me an early lesson about interviewing people: don't let them talk. It was fine for Parkinson to earn his money with a raised eyebrow and the odd prompt, but Parky's guests had stuff to say. Betty, who did not, talked for hours. And herein lay the deeper lesson: without really registering this at the time, I wanted, deep down, for her to be erased, or at least attenuated, and for me, my part, my introduction, my summing-up, to be, as Donald Trump would put it, 'huge'.

Narcissism. We joke about it. Actors are accused of being driven by it. Lesser performers, radio presenters, perhaps, are said to have it in spades, even if their artistic merits are fewer. But having it might not be so comfortable. It is, in some respects, a curse. Or a sign of a derangement that has been visited upon the narcissistic person.

My early life was dominated by the need to please and the need to conceal; to be someone I was not without letting anyone know what was going on. Running parallel with the love my mother so selflessly and totally provided, the love that nurtured her child as all children should be nurtured, there was a set of expectations that had their own impact. These expectations were not a policy she consciously pursued as she struggled with what life had dealt her but, alongside that love, I was carrying twin burdens. First, I was acutely aware that my mother was unhappy, that her life was less than it should be and that, if there was any one single key to her being all right, it was me. I needed to be wonderful. Everything depended on it.

So if anything went wrong, it had to be hidden. 'Suppressed' would be the word a therapist would use: a conscious, almost calculated approach to life that turns significant emotional areas of it into a performance. In (the very few) moments of falling out between Mum and me – childhood tantrums or arguments – my mind would always take me straight beyond normal boundaries into a world of catastrophizing. What if she died tonight? What if I did? Would either of us ever be able to pick up the pieces?

We walked on eggshells at 90 Wells Road. A child gets used to that sensation. You learn how to shift your way through life without creating even the tiniest crunch, even if you might occasionally want to. Anger, in particular, is banished. Mum, to my intense embarrassment, once told a friend that she couldn't understand the fuss people made about teenagers and bad behaviour (punk rock was just getting going) as 'Justin has never gone through that stage at all.' Well, no. I hardly could, I might have said. That stage was not available to me. Sure, it was lovely to be grown up and to be praised for being grown up, but sustaining the act took its toll. The audience appreciation was nice, but some time off the stage would have been nice, too, and, in the long term, probably rather beneficial.

To claim narcissism as a clinical diagnosis for myself – a psychological neediness as reaction to the oddness of my early life – would be, er, narcissistic and, in spite of the metaphor I have just used, I am certainly not going to do that. But all of us who seek attention from an early age, in particular those who are troubled at the same time, might be advised to face the fact that this is not normal and not healthy. The risk is that you actually turn into the performer you had to be. Criticism from people close to you becomes hard to take, or more personally wounding than it should be. The problem is not that you like praise (who doesn't?) but that something broader than praise – admiration – develops into a drug. Or perhaps a cloak. And, in your desire to be at the top of every tree, you become more unpleasant than you want to be. The aphorism attributed to Somerset Maugham and Gore Vidal, among others, 'It's not enough that I succeed, my friends must fail', is funny when you first hear it. But is it? If you really think that (and I have, I admit), what does it say about you? And what does it do to you? Some of the happiest people I know are focused on others. Having children of your own helps: it drives the grandiosity out of you. In fact, in the modern, child-centred world, it goes further. It forces you to make a choice: you or them?

When I look back at my letters from school, amid the sadness and the amusing stories and the genuine sense of achievement that any child would write to any parent about, there is something else: a pact between mother and child that speaks of exclusivity and, that word again, performance. 'I have won my first prize at Sidcot', rather than 'I have won a prize'. And for whom was this prize won? For me, on one level, for sure. I loved nothing more than applause. But mostly for her. To enable me to bask in her affection but, more corrosively, to assuage her unhappiness, perhaps her sense of guilt.

Even the saddest of letters in my first years at Sidcot were models of delicacy. 'Thanks for taking me out yesterday. I was feeling very depressed but I am much better now. I shall write some poems today and have a rest. I am looking forward to your letter tomorrow.'

In another, written the day after coming back to school after a leave afternoon back in Bath: 'Sorry I left a mess in my room. We had to leave so suddenly.' But never down for long. 'I am having a super time. My new dorm is much nicer and I am warm in bed. We start work on Monday. My radio is admired by everyone.'

Those poems, oh, Lord! I was so proud of them but they were written entirely for her. They contained the feelings I knew *she* had. As a militant peacenik she liked attacks on warriors best and, if not the warriors themselves, then on the institutions that served them. This one appeared in the school magazine in 1974.

A man of the church
Told me to love my neighbour
A man of the same church
Told me to fight for my country
A man of still the same church
Told me to love my enemies
A man also of that church
Told me to triumph over my enemies
I'm very confused.

It has all Mum's pet hates: men, churches, nations, war. Only the working classes are missing. I am sure I was genuinely pacific in my young tastes but this is the opposite of youthful free thinking. Emotionally, intellectually, I was captured. These were poems written by a hostage. A zoo animal; a performing monkey.

8

The Magic Bus

Should I buy swimming trunks or would my underwear –
tight-fitting stripy briefs of a type never fashionable
anywhere ever – suffice? I went for the underwear option
because, although I was going on a journey, certainly life-
changing, possibly life-enhancing, I was still not properly
functioning in the world. We had kept ourselves so aloof,
Mum and I. So sophisticated, we told ourselves, when
compared to the terrible Burgesses or to the folk on the
coach trips. But they would have bought swimming trunks
without a second thought. It was partly money – we were
at this stage quite poor and worried about getting poorer –
but mostly it was an inability to be normal, to be ready for
fun, to be relaxed enough to think, 'I might swim.' I could
pronounce words, denounce oppressive regimes, question
the need for schools, hold my knife and fork as com-
petently as any member of any royal family, but I was

confounded by the task of equipping myself with the basic kit for a trip abroad.

This failure to buy the trunks took place in Exeter. Mum had moved, with Charles, to a house in nearby Budleigh Salterton. Pebble-beached Budleigh, peopled by stiff-limbed retirees on comfortable index-linked, final-salary pensions, described (correctly) as a place where the young couldn't live and the old couldn't die. Mum had decided to make a break for some kind of freedom. Her rebellious outer persona relished the chance to live among the former stockbrokers while disliking and disparaging them. Her rather more conventional inner persona probably fancied a rest and a choice of butchers' shops, much as they did. Her sister, Charmion, had lived in Budleigh Salterton for years and provided an infrastructure of sorts. There could be walks by the sea. Charles, though still in tow, was now hugely diminished, physically frail and confused. He had a room on the ground floor of the house with a view of a small back garden ending in the embankment of a disused railway, an old branch line long overgrown by nettles.

What a year that was, its futuristic numerals – 1980 – freighted with the promise of fizzing modernity after the moribund and sclerotic 1970s, cloth-capped and coal-powered. We were going nuclear: Mrs Thatcher at the helm and the ship of state heading for all manner of purposeful clashes. An end to the meandering, meaningless distress that had seen us fighting the waves, bobbing unsteadily from rock to rock. Now we were simply heading straight for them: tally ho! Socially, of course, the idea that we might take charge of ourselves, shape our destinies, sail our own ships, all tended to have an effect that Mrs Thatcher and her crew had not fully grasped. As individuals we were freed to break out and become who we wanted to be. To swell the ranks in London clubs of the punk rockers or the New Romantics, chaps in make-up and girls in boiler suits, as 2-Tone music (the Specials, the Selecter, Madness) played loud across the land. The 2-Tone genre originated in Coventry, of all places, a city that was famous mainly for having been flattened by German bombers in the war forty years previously. Now there was energy, and it came from scallywags with little formal education, scallywags careless as to how they held their knives and forks or enunciated the Queen's English. Mum had never wanted to join the conventional set, the social conservatives, but when it came to it, in those heady days at the end of the decade, she was just as firmly swept aside as a bewigged judge or stuffy, bowler-hatted stockbroker.

A wave was breaking. There was a kind of inevitability about the change. More than inevitability: the word is too passive. It fails to capture the profound force of what was happening. After the stasis of the seventies, all the confusion and dust-flecked depression, something unstoppable by any human hand was taking shape. Just as the laws of thermodynamics tell us that heat cannot pass from a cooler object to a hotter one, we were locked, after years of drift, into a state decreed by something as inexorable, as fundamental, as physics. We were on our way. There was no room for argument. There was only one way to go.

I began the year in a Black & Decker factory in Maidenhead. I had gone to live in nearby Reading in a room provided for free by Sue Curtis, a young drama teacher who had just left Sidcot, and her husband Martin. It was an extraordinarily generous offer. It allowed me to be free from home and to earn good money putting small electric currents through broken power tools and, if they didn't show any life, chucking them in a giant bin. Eight hours a day. In our lunch breaks we would sit amid the forklift trucks and talk about football. I had never spent so much time among properly working-class people in my life before. I expected them to be resentful of my university future, my education, my accent. Of course, they couldn't have given a monkey's. This was still the era of mass university non-attendance and of real class division. They were not really interested. Very few knew anyone who was going to university. When I looked at them I realized that poverty was not what separated us – in fact they were probably all better off than I had ever been. It was the comparative certainty they could have, at a young age, about what the future held. They were not going anywhere. They were not intending to or even wanting to.

The oldest of them would have made a wonderful teacher. Thoughtful and twinkly-eyed Ray drove a forklift truck (this was an aristocratic role on the shop floor). He had worked at the factory all his life. 'I came here to get out of the rain,' he told me one lunchtime. We laughed at that. He and I gave blood that day, sitting together in the makeshift surgery next to the giant bins full of drills while the nurses fussed around and the more squeamish louts peered around them, half horrified, half envious.

'Are you going to be prime minister?' Ray asked as we sipped our sweet tea afterwards and milked the time we could legitimately spend 'resting' before going back to work.

'Perhaps.'

Oh, Ray. You were joking but I was serious. You had the advantage, and the disadvantage, of having lived life. I had the advantage, and the disadvantage, of not having done a thing. Ray confused me: all of my upbringing had positioned me in this relationship as master, albeit the young master, and him as servant, in the thrall of the boss class to which, in spite of impecuniousness, I belonged. Actually, I think Ray felt for me a bit. He saw me for what I was: a rather eccentric specimen of young humanity. Not to be envied, particularly, but not pitied, either. What would he have made of 90 Wells Road? Of my stepfather? The driving lessons with Mum, the holiday in Croyde Bay, the coach obsession, the shambolic Quaker school? I think he'd have raised an eyebrow but made no judgement. We didn't need to judge any more: by 1980 the working classes could learn to live alongside distressed gentlefolk and I could learn to be with Ray. He didn't judge me and, somewhere in my subconscious, I think I learned not to judge him, though, at that stage, I would never have said so to Mum.

The reason for the factory work was the collection of sufficient funds for my trip. The big journey which was going to mark the end of my childhood. In the summer I was intending to break free on a grand scale. The InterRail pass had been invented and the whole of Europe beckoned. Martin and Sue Curtis were going to be staying on an island near Athens and the plan was for me to set off from there and criss-cross Europe by train back to Budleigh Salterton. I would do it alone because it never occurred to me to do it any other way.

And so, newly returned from Reading and the factory with enough money saved to buy my ticket, here I was, at the shops in Exeter with Mum, preparing to go. A basic rucksack and a jacket with large pockets. No swimming trunks. The ingredients for nut roast.

This was in the days before anything was easy. Although I was a meticulous planner there was no way that I would be in anything like constant contact with Mum, or with Sue and Martin. Postcards, the odd call from a phone box. That was it. We lived apart from each other. We did not know what others were doing at any given moment of the day, of the week. We still wrote letters. This journey was a big deal, then, for me and for Mum.

In 1980 there was one young person's InterRail pass option, which offered unlimited second-class travel across Europe for a month. Mine was timed to start on my departure from Greece. First I had to get there on a tight budget. This was the age of the bus: the Magic Bus. Three and a half days to Greece from Victoria coach station. Roughly. Nothing promised – not even the departure time, which was subject to negotiation. You had to call the office the day before to find out when the coach was likely to be leaving. But £30 would get you a one-way ticket: London, Antwerp, Paris, Lyons, Milan, Venice, Zagreb, Belgrade, Thessaloniki, Athens. Bring your own food and a sleeping bag. The coach would stop occasionally but only briefly – our estimated arrival time was reliant on solid driving throughout those three and a half days, and the nights in between. 'Trips are casual,' the flyers advised, 'the coaches are sturdy but are not new or air-conditioned.' The drivers, they said, 'are young Europeans and are usually mechanics as well'.

On 2 August I hugged Mum and left Budleigh Salterton. To all intents and purposes, I had left home at the age of eleven, and again in the early months of the year to make money at Black & Decker, but this felt more final. It almost was.

London in 1980 was a dump. A mere forty years back, at the beginning of the Second World War, it had been the biggest city in the world. But the war took its obvious toll and the revivification of the swinging sixties never quite returned it to its past glory. It had staggered through the seventies with little enclaves of regeneration but no real sense of common purpose. It had no pride. Londoners were moving out. Shops and businesses were closing. It wasn't as crime-ridden and dangerous as New York but it was grimy and ropey. People, on balance, preferred Hemel Hempstead. London was down on its luck and nobody expected that to change. So, for me, the bleakness of the big city was not a shock – this was how it was universally portrayed and, of course, I had visited it once before, on our Anti-Nazi League and porn-film expedition, and sampled a bit of the grime for myself – but it still felt strange to be there alone, wandering around Victoria coach station, waiting to embark on a journey away from any life I had known. In a place where dangers unknown in the Mendips might lurk.

There was a deadness in the eyes of Londoners in those days. The cigarettes didn't help: the top floors of the old Routemaster buses were filled with billows of yellowing smoke. The vibe of the whole city was cancerous. The cafés poisonous-looking, serving chips and omelettes on dirty plates. The tube trains, metal-floored, museum-quality but still in service. In fact the whole place was still trundling along on ancient wheels, half belonging to a distant age. Everything was patched: nothing had been replaced or refreshed since the old days.

Mum had told me once about the journey home on a number 11 bus from the *Daily Mirror* offices in Fleet Street to her rented bedsit after she lost her job at the paper. When she had announced to the bosses that she was pregnant they had sacked her on the spot. She had given no more detail but the description had made me angry at the injustice and sad, too, affected by the poignancy of the scene she had briskly described: lurching home on that bus, friendless, through darkening streets. At Victoria, as the afternoon wore on and I waited for my coach, I saw bus after bus going in direction after direction. And then, just as I was meandering between the train station and the coach park, a number 11.

Yes, I had cycled alone to East Coker but this aloneness felt different.

The Magic Bus was a lie. There was no magic and no specific bus. The company simply hired coaches as needed or bought space on other services. Lesson number one of the trip: con artists and dodgy sales people are not the preserve of big business. Multinationals might behave badly but so could people with long hair and weed-filled cigarettes. The Magic Bus conjured up an image of a small outfit that was 'sticking it to the man' and therefore wholly decent. In fact it was neither: it was a nakedly commercial enterprise that put young people in desperate danger. Even less trustworthy than the faceless multinationals because no large company could have got away with it.

I didn't know anything about the danger, as we pulled out into the south London traffic, but I felt uneasy, with my rucksack next to me and my seat, halfway down the coach, a little harder than I expected. In the row in front of me, a woman in her twenties, blonde hair and military fatigues, talked to herself softly in Greek as we squeaked and juddered through Camberwell, Peckham, assorted other bedraggled south London neighbourhoods and then, finally, on to the motorway to Dover, which the driver took at speed, as if we were late already.

On the deck of the ferry, briefly liberated from my unforgiving seat, I tried to be excited but what I felt in the pit of my stomach was something more like fear. The gusts of wind blocked out all other sounds. The sea, green and evil-looking, heaved around us as we ploughed towards Calais. It was getting dark as we arrived. There was no turning back now, an inevitability to every aspect of this journey. Nobody spoke as we clambered back on the bus. We were off, for me, for the first time ever, on the wrong side of the road.

We made Paris at midnight but it wasn't quite the Paris I had read about. It was a bus station far from the centre, in some godforsaken banlieu. It was chilly and I felt very alone and very aware of a sensation I have had so many times since. We are mixtures, are we not, of fortitude and fear. Of explorer and homebird. And we blend these characteristics in our own appreciation of ourselves. Was I, am I, a seeker after the thrill of the new? Kind of. But, as I looked around that bus garage and smelled the loos and watched the girl who had been talking to herself being sick against the wheel of another bus, I also hankered after Budleigh Salterton. The same feeling came over me decades later, in a column of Egyptian troops heading into Kuwait on the night the first Gulf War began. Is this me? What the hell am I doing here?

There was no going back, in either Kuwait or France. We reached the Alps some time during the next day, by which point a sort of catatonic silence had descended on the whole coach. People slept or gazed out of the window and stretched and grazed on the food they had been enjoined to bring in order not to be ripped off by expensive cafés at the bus stations en route. I had some nut roast near Lyons and wondered about what life held in store for me.

It is extraordinary that any of these coaches ever reached their destinations. The drivers (the advertised 'young Europeans' who were 'usually mechanics as well') were unsmiling, pot-bellied, middle-aged men who spoke only Greek and whose sole mission appeared to be to get back to Greece as soon as possible, as if it were due only to some giant mistake that they had ever left. Nor did they like the look of the company they were forced to keep. I knew only the jolly drivers of Roman City Coaches with their mild teasing of the folk from Peasedown St John. These men looked through their passengers and, when addressed in anything other than Greek, shrugged and turned away. There were three of them but only two ever drove: was the other one on strike? I wondered (it was still close enough to the 1970s for that vibe to be strong). Perhaps he was merely hitching a lift with his co-workers. Perhaps he couldn't actually drive.

In truth, none of them could. A tiny, grizzled man did most of what passed for driving, pushing the coach through its gears and right up to the very brake lights of anything in front, before hitting his own brakes, slowing down and repeating the manoeuvre. A very fat colleague in a stained white T-shirt and huge jeans would take over at the wheel for a bit from time to time, on straight bits of road, which involved some footwork that made even the most catatonic of us blink. Grizzled Driver would get the coach into fourth gear and lurch suddenly out of his seat while keeping one hand on the wheel. The coach was coasting along with no ability to brake. Fat Man would ease himself into the seat and grab the wheel, slightly correcting a course that was taking us into the middle of the road. He would hit the brake to see if it worked, then power on. The drivers did not sleep and did not eat. By the time we got close to the Yugoslavian border, they looked in worse nick than the passengers.

That border was still a proper east–west divide, a transition from freedom to communism, albeit the slightly relaxed regime of Tito rather than the proper Soviet Bloc. Still, it entailed a full-scale passport check. The guards wore those greatcoats you see in spy films. As they moved through the vehicle, they spoke to each passenger. I was used to handling officialdom with the breezy arrogance my mother had taught me. Not here. 'You have hashish, we kill you,' they said as they eyed my nut roast. I could find no answer.

They passed on. And, shifting my position to turn slightly, I watched a trifling scene unfold which I have often thought about down the years. A man sitting two or three rows behind me, a neatly dressed guy not much older than me, was asleep against the seat in front. When the guards roused him he woke with a start and jumped up to find his bag. After giving them his passport, I saw him realize that he had biscuit crumbs down his shirt and, presumably, all over his seat. So he moved places and sat down in the empty seat in front. Such a small thing at the time. *Sliding Doors* again.

There was one main road through Yugoslavia. I have seen it described as a motorway but that's not how I remember it. More of a track in some places, with huge queues of vehicles waiting to pass over an unpaved, puddle-strewn wasteland before rejoining the main carriageway. And it was single-carriageway all the way – one lane down to Greece and the other bringing traffic into western Europe. It was afternoon and it was hot: my first taste of southern European heat. Grizzled Driver was at the wheel and in his groove, pulling out to overtake tractors and lorries and back into our lane just in time, or sometimes a little late, judging by the loud hooting of offended oncoming vehicles, which faded as we sped on. He seemed to know what he was doing, even if what he was doing was dangerous. Perhaps this was adult life. Perhaps this was the life I wanted to lead.

Anyone who has been involved in a serious road accident will know the sense of sickly certainty you feel in the milliseconds before the impact; a certainty that all is going to change and any opportunity to stop it changing has gone.

We were on a decent bit of road. Proper tarmac, even white lines in the middle. The carriageway was raised about a metre higher than the fields on each side. As far as the eye could see was flat farmland. The driver had pulled out to overtake but either he had misjudged the engine or the gear or the gradient, or something had not responded as expected. The coach just didn't produce the power needed to get past a local bus. We were probably doing 40 or 50mph. And, hurtling towards us, at a similar speed, was a lorry.

I saw it all in slow motion. The wheel yanked in a vain attempt to get us on to an impossibly small pathway beside the road and above the field. The looming embankment. The slow turning of the vehicle in mid-air. My seat was on the left of the coach, on the same side as the driver. Round we went, and crunch, we landed. The force of the landing did two things in perfect order. First, it shattered the window next to me. Then it threw me out of my seat, propelling me through the window where the glass had been. I found myself on my feet, standing in the field. Around me were several other passengers, lying on the ground or sitting, dazed.

Smoke, wheels spinning, silence. No one screamed or even spoke.

Then came moaning from inside the vehicle. People were still in there and fuel from the ruptured tank was dripping on them. We pulled them out. Spotting my rucksack, I pulled that out, too.

And the man behind me who had changed places? He was crumpled where he had been sleeping, against a stanchion separating two windows. It had crushed him. I am not sure any of us got close enough to check, but he was clearly dead, his body contorted and broken.

It was hot. We gathered under a tree. Up on the road the traffic slowed down to look but carried on. Other buses paused, their passengers staring down at us. Several cars stopped and people brought us water. Eventually – it must have been hours later – the British consul arrived, incongruously wearing a tan suit, accompanied by his wife, who was dressed in white. I suppose they'd had to come straight from some diplomatic do.

It was filmic. Assuming, in my shocked state, that this was how Britons were always rescued in scrapes abroad, I felt absurdly proud of my country as we sat there with the consul taking notes and arranging for transport to the hospital and to local hotels. I have no idea who this man actually was or why he was there that afternoon but whenever anyone uses the term 'British diplomat', the first image that pops into my mind is of him.

The drivers had scarpered. God knows where they went, since we really were in the middle of nowhere and Yugoslavia was a pretty tricky nation to get in and out of without being noticed. But they knew not only that the passengers would blame them, rightly, for the crash, but that the government of Yugoslavia was quite capable of chucking them in jail and throwing away the key. Perhaps they had been in this situation before. Whatever the case, they had gone. I had never in my life come across any situation from which adults had simply run away. Except metaphorically, of course, which had happened all the time back in Bath. To see this occurring, here and now, for real, in real time, was astounding.

In that field, as the afternoon wore on, we chatted about life and celebrated still being here to live it. When we looked back at the coach, upside down on the roadside, we experienced what I now know to be the feeling you always get after narrowly avoided calamities: surges of pure sugar-rush joy, followed by listless bewilderment at the horror of it all. Our eyes strayed constantly to that coach, with the man in it who could have been any of us, who was one of us, and who was dead.

Lesson number two came from that field: book learning combined with street wisdom is an insuperable force. We were split into groups. First those who needed to get to hospital were taken off. The rest of us were to be housed in nearby hotels while a replacement bus was sent from Greece. It would take days, probably, but it was the best that could be done. The hell it was. A man not much older than me, dressed rather expensively and elegantly in black, Greek but speaking perfect English, begged to differ. 'I'm off,' he said. 'Come with me, if you want.'

Stelios, who turned out to be a student at the London School of Economics, was afraid of flying but, it seemed, of nothing else. He was on his way back to Greece having completed the first year of his doctorate in econometric methods. From the coach he had rescued a book entitled *Stochastic Orders of Magnitude*. Those terms – econometric methods and stochastic orders of magnitude – have stuck with me for a lifetime, though I have no more idea now what they mean than I did then, under the thorny shelter of a tree in a Yugoslav field.

But he was more than a scholar. Stelios was also a proper southern European, schooled in the ways of the continent and knowledge of the areas where street wisdom properly pays. 'We get off the bus in the town, and we slip away,' he whispered to me. 'We find a station, get on a train, and we can be in Athens by tomorrow night.'

Which is precisely what we did. It was eye-opening moment after eye-opening moment for a boy freshly out of Wells Road, freshly out of boarding school. We located a train track and followed it to a station, which seemed to be lacking the ticket barriers and stern warnings about fare-dodging that were customary back at home. In fact, there was no question of tickets at all, let alone any need to reserve a seat, as I had made sure to do for the Exeter to London journey, properly in advance. Stelios found us a train going south. We pushed our way on board and squatted in the stinking corridor next to compartments jammed with peasants and students and animals, dead and alive. We had no tickets and were never asked for them.

Yugoslavia was over. Greece arrived with the dawn. And eventually, Athens. 'See ya,' Stelios said.

And that was that. Nowadays there would be a Facebook group for those of us who survived that journey. We would have kept in touch for years. We would have written about it and discussed it. As an event it would have stayed alive because we would have kept it alive, just as people who die are kept alive by being talked about by those they leave behind. But in those days: nothing, really. We all melted away. You can still find very brief reports of the crash in newspaper cuttings if you search online but there is nothing more. Completely by accident, Stelios and I bumped into each other years later at the LSE but the experience had not bound us and we had no other reason to stay in touch.

I took a ferry the short distance to the island of Aegina, where I was several days late for my rendezvous with Martin and Sue, with whom I was meant to be lodging. I had no way of contacting them and no idea where, on the island, they were staying. Here there was no one to enforce the sleep with which we launched, many years before, the disastrous holiday in Croyde Bay. No out-of-place singing, no social-class minefields to negotiate. No Charles. No Mum. As soon as I arrived, I went to the beach, stripped off down to that stripy underwear and walked into the sea. I was exhausted and suffering from shock. I still couldn't swim properly but I experimented with my breaststroke in the shallows, where small children played around me.

When my briefs were dry again I put my jeans back on and strolled into the small town. I saw Martin and Sue coming down the hill as I walked up it. A third important lesson: coincidences happen in life. And, if you think about it, the chances of you bumping into someone you know in an area where you are both intending to be are not so small. Be resourceful and hopeful. Believe things might turn out OK.*

A month after the Yugoslavia crash, I got back to Britain and took the train down to Exeter and the bus to Budleigh. For dramatic effect I did not call ahead. I just turned up, a returning soldier at the end of a life-changing war. We ate sausages. Several things had happened. Charles had died. I had been accepted into a hall of residence called International Students House, a glamorous-sounding place to start life in London. Auntie Charmion, her husband long dead, had taken up with a local garage-owner, in considerable contravention of class laws. But maybe they didn't matter any more. Mum also had a new life ahead of her: a life of freedom from her husband and freedom from her son, who was ready to face the world.

We had one more joint task. One more private piece of unfinished business. Charles had a wardrobe, a huge, dark-stained lump of Edwardian furniture. It had creaking double doors and four bulbous legs. It smelled, not unpleasantly,

---

* Years later, a lifetime later, in the first Gulf War, I was in the middle of the desert, despairing of meeting up with some colleagues who had a satellite dish in their Jeep. In the distance we could hear the thunder of an American bombing raid. All around us were dunes; next to us, by the road, a kind of asbestos hut, painted white, that was probably used for shelter in sandstorms. I had a bottle of tomato ketchup in my vehicle (we had been taught by the army to travel with essentials) and I used it to smear a message on the side of the hut telling my colleagues where in Kuwait we were heading.

A day later they came by and saw it, and by that evening they had found us.

of sandalwood and desiccated emptiness. But it was the smell of him. Of the life we had lived. He had taken the wardrobe with him to Bruton when all went wrong in London. Then, along with his new wife, to The Beeches, scene of the boats-versus-boots debacle, and on to Wells Road, where it had been miraculously shoehorned into the tiny bedroom. And, finally, to Budleigh and his room overlooking the railway embankment.

Mum and I dismembered it. We sawed it up. I wonder why she didn't sell it. Or perhaps I don't really wonder. We laughed as we sawed. The top of the wardrobe came off in one piece and we took it outside to complete the job. In my haste I cut myself on the saw and spots of blood stained the wood and the ground. When we snapped the lighter wood, elderly ply, that formed the back, it seemed to burst. Dust everywhere. Ancient dust. Danger of splinters.

We had survived.

∾

Three years later, nearly at the end of my university life, the postman called while I was still asleep. I woke to screams from my housemates in our dingy west London basement. They had opened (with my permission, given while drunk, I think) a letter I was expecting from the BBC. It informed me that I had been accepted on to the graduate training scheme for journalists. This scheme was widely regarded in those days as the fast track to success.

A few months later I bought a blue shirt with a collar and some chinos (not a bad guess at the BBC uniform, it turned out) and caught the number 14 bus to Piccadilly, walking up Regent Street to Broadcasting House.

In a room at the BBC headquarters that day I met Jeremy Bowen, who was to become a lifelong friend, and another six seekers after the fame and semi-fortune the corporation offered. It was another age. We were all white, all highly educated, mostly at Oxbridge or the bigger London colleges. We were each given a desk with a typewriter. We were taken on trips around the country and taught to embellish our expenses in the old-fashioned way. We visited the army in Germany. We learned shorthand which we would never use. I can still write 'all over the world' in a fast Teeline shortcut, though no one has ever said those words to me and time is running out. Still, the whole experience was glamorous in a seedy, faded kind of way. The men (oh, yes, they were all men) who ran the course were amiable newsroom characters who had been put out to grass. One of them told us he had been on the foreign desk the night Turkey invaded Cyprus. It had been quite a night, he said.

Our eyes widened politely. This was still an age of deference in the BBC as it was in the wider world. But in truth we were unimpressed. We wanted to be actually in Cyprus, or wherever the latest action might be, wearing a flak jacket. We had read the veteran foreign correspondent Ed Behr's book *Anyone Here Been Raped and Speaks English?*

and various other tales of reporting bravado and derring-do. Jeremy and I had ambitions already to be out there dodging the bullets and getting the girl. On the day they taught us to back-time the news bulletin so as to come out on the dot – an essential part of the journey that would lead to the job of producer, then senior producer, then editor and perhaps, one day, director-general – Jeremy and I caught each other's eye and knew immediately we were thinking the same thing: this was not for us. We wanted to be front of house. On stage. Not fumbling about behind the scenes making sure the curtain fell at the right moment and getting a credit that flashed on the screen for no more than a second. We were destined for something else, something better, we decided.

There was, of course, another potential role model available to ambitious broadcasters in the early 1980s. In his earlier life he had made a parachute landing into Suez, he had been there when the Berlin Wall went up, he had interviewed Martin Luther King in Alabama. He had become, as you still could in the 1970s, in a world of three channels on the telly, a genuine household name. It would have been odd to meet anyone who did not recognize his face.

I never thought about him. This was not suppression, a deliberate and conscious decision. It was repression. My awareness of my father had been forced so deep it never came anywhere near the surface. So deep it was gone. It was not even there to be considered. Peter Woods had left the BBC in 1981. We had coincided in London for a year while I had been at university. He had been retired for three years when I first walked into a TV newsroom. I knew neither of those things at the time because it honestly never occurred to me to take an interest in them. London was a big place. We had lives to lead.

Perhaps that was eccentric; perhaps it was just par for the course for a child of the 1970s. The philosopher John Gray tells us that humans turned to philosophy largely out of anxiety. When the world is inexplicable we look for meaning. But in the search we damage ourselves because there is no meaning to be found, or at least none we can see. We should live like cats, he tells us in his bestselling book *Feline Philosophy: Cats and the Meaning of Life.* In common with much philosophical work, his big insight is quite obvious when you think about it. The trick is to have thought about it.

Gray points out that cats don't think about being cats. This is the key to their joy. This is why they are superior to us. They are engaged in their lives without getting too fussed – or fussed at all – about who they are, what others think of them, whether they should have been kinder or tougher. Taken this road or that. They certainly don't go on about being lonely.

In the 1970s we were not thrilled, not driven as we are now, by what we thought of as our own identities. Introspection was for losers or French philosophers. We still had a bit of the cat about us. We did not, yet, overthink our role in the world or in our nation. In our relations with each other, in our families, we made the best of bad lots without feeling ... well, that there was anything we could do to change things. And, for all the coal dust and decay, the political collapse, the existential national angst, we still felt somehow moored to something. For millions it was the union (how quickly we forget what a part they played in the life of the country) or the Church or the political party (also still boasting mass membership), or, as for Mum, social class, mixed – paradoxically, as I am sure she'd have admitted – with the progressive politics of social change. I was tied, for better or worse, to Sidcot School.

But all our ties were fraying. For my generation, individualism was invented at the precise moment we became adult, which was particularly dizzying, even without the added weirdness of 90 Wells Road and poor old Charles and his padlocks. It was nice to escape the 1970s, to have survived them, but the revisionist historians of the era are probably right: it was not all bad. Even in our confusion we had, as one of the maudlin songs of the time put it, 'seasons in the sun'. We are much better at expressing ourselves these days; we have burst free, but in bursting, given ourselves a whole host of new anxieties about how to use that freedom and how angry we should be when it seems not to lead to happiness. In truth, none of us is liberated from our past. We cannot be. It is, to use that mildly annoying American phrase, what it is.

I look back with amazement, with affection, with relief, and I wouldn't change a thing.

Through my life the memories have come in waves, blowing in with the wind, with the distant mental sketch of a day at the beach, a stepfather who did not drown; with the question from a child: 'Daddy, why don't you have a daddy?'

A decade ago, when my children were young, our family pitched our towels on Lyme Regis beach near a woman whose small son was playing in front of her. It was cold and only the hardiest were venturing into the water. He wanted to, her little boy, but she told him to be *sensible*. That word brought a physical sensation of being transported back in time. My reaction was one you only normally see in cartoons: mouth opened to say something but nothing coming out.

What could I have said? Don't worry, it'll be OK?

When Tolstoy told us that 'all happy families are alike; every unhappy family is unhappy in its own way', we understand that he meant all the bits and pieces have to fall roughly into place to bring happiness, and it is the absence of one bit – not always the same bit – that dooms the enterprise. How right he was but how wrong to fix it in such binary terms. My unhappy family was unhappy because of the lack of a father but also because of the sadness of a mother and the failings of a son. But sometimes it was fine. One person's love can be enough. I have had more fun laughing at the *Morecambe and Wise* show, or gliding down Dartmoor hills in the front seat of a Roman City coach, than many people whose earlier lives might be considered more blessed or more secure.

And, Lord knows, any life has its grim moments. You take an average, don't you? Or you don't think about it at all: one of the benefits of the stiff upper lip employed by Mum, and her whole generation of postwar distressed gentlefolk, is that you significantly reduce the time spent analysing these things. Most of the gloomiest moments of my childhood were those when I stopped to consider my life. Socrates said an unexamined life was not worth living. Well, all right, but maybe do the examining only towards the end. Better to be John Gray's cat until then.

Peter Woods and I never met. But one of the blessings of an eccentric upbringing is that it frees you from conventional regret. He had children he loved. They loved him. I had a mother I loved, who loved me.

In the end, what else is there?

Acknowledgements

I am immensely grateful to friends of my mother still living in the city of Bath who have spoken to me about their memories of her, and of the muesli-filled, tie-dyed, hessian-wallpaper-lined lives they led in the 1970s. Several are still working for world peace and I hope they achieve it. Special mention should be made of Nick and Diana Francis, serious lifelong campaigners with a sense of humour: both features that always greatly endeared them to Mum and to me. Thanks, too, to Doris Fenna and her family and to my wonderfully accomplished cousin Gregory Woods.

Patrick Southall was my closest friend at school and has come up with countless useful details from the yacht on which he lives, far from us all. Jonathan Berg and Adrian Chalker have also been generous with time and memories, as have Helen and John Argyropoulos, Tom Leimdorfer, Martin Bell, and Caroline Lane. Huge thanks, too, to Mandy Elliot and to innumerable fellow Sidcotians. I salute the many friends of ours who have, in spite of (or because of) our haphazard education, created good lives and brought joy to others. Some of the events at school I have jumbled and altered to protect identities but even allowing for these devices I cannot stress enough that the assessments made of my mother, my step-father and of Sidcot are mine and mine alone. The modern school appears to me to bear no resemblance to the old; in this book I am talking about another country, a foreign country.

I am also grateful to Owen and Mandy Bennett Jones and to Jeremy and Astrid James, with whom I lived in great happiness in my first years in London.

I am deeply indebted to my literary agent, Toby Mundy, whose idea this book was, and to Susanna Wadeson, who has been the most supportive and encouraging publisher it's possible to have. The entire experience of working with her and her team – in particular Patsy Irwin, Lucy Middleton, Caroline North McIlvanney, Richard Ogle and Sharika Teelwah – has been nothing but pleasurable.

I should acknowledge, too, my enormous debt of gratitude to my half-brother Guy and his family for their forbearance and for their friendship.

Thanks to my children, Sam, Martha and Clara; I am proud of the people they have become and happy to be a source of amusement to them, I hope for years to come. And endless thanks to my wife, Sarah, the girl I met and fell in love with at Jeremy Bowen's party all those years ago, when the events in this book were a relatively recent memory, who saw me as someone worth knowing, worth rescuing from all this nonsense.

Text Acknowledgements

Pages 12–13: Philip Larkin's words are from his poem 'This Be the Verse', published in *High Windows* (Faber & Faber, 1974).

Page 75: Pablo Neruda's words are from 'Every Day You Play', published in *Selected Poems* (Vintage Classics, 2012).

Page 76: Stevie Smith's words are from 'Not Waving But Drowning', published in *The Collected Poems and Drawings of Stevie Smith* (Faber & Faber, 2015).

Pages 86–7: Alastair Campbell is quoted from his article 'This is how my crippling depression feels', published in *GQ* magazine, 1 September 2020.

Page 146: Lyrics from 'The Jean Genie' on the album *Aladdin Sane* by David Bowie (David Bowie, 1972).

Page 155: Philip Larkin's words are from his poem 'Annus Mirabilis', published in *High Windows* (Faber & Faber, 1974).

Page 155: Lyrics from 'All Right Now' on the album *Fire and Water* by Free (Andy Fraser/Paul Rodgers, 1970).

Page 167: Lyrics from 'Oh Daddy' on the album *Rumours* by Fleetwood Mac (Christine McVie, 1976).

Page 181: The full letter from Albert Camus to his former teacher, Monsieur Germain, is published in *More Letters of Note* (Unbound, 2015).

Page 186: Robert Frost's words are from 'The Gift Outright' from *The Poetry of Robert Frost*, edited by Edward Connery Lathem. Copyright 1923, © 1969 by Henry Holt and Company, Inc., renewed 1951, by Robert Frost.